GRACE, NOTED

BY

Jane Marshall

COMPILED AND EDITED BY

Rosemary Heffley

FOREWORD BY

Natalie Sleeth

Code No. 956

Hope Publishing Company
CAROL STREAM IL 60188

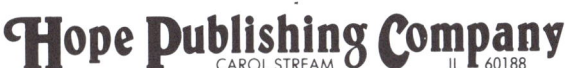

Copyright © 1992 by Hope Publishing Company
All Rights Reserved. International Copyright Secured.
Printed in the U.S.A.
Library of Congress Catalog Card Number: 92-070255
ISBN 0-916642-45-3

Foreword

I have known Jane Marshall since the mid-'60s, when we both sang alto in the Dallas Civic Chorus under the direction of Dr. Lloyd Pfautsch, and I have always admired and respected her as a composer of singable, sensitive, and well-written church music. I see in this book, however, Jane Marshall as preacher, teacher, and poet, as well.

Her knowledge of the Bible and her understanding of its relevance for all of us, but especially for musicians, are unquestionably present in her "Stories of Grace," which are thought-provoking, theologically challenging, and beautifully readable. Based on the Common Lectionary, many of these are sermons she has preached in worship services where she has doubled as visiting choir director.

Jane Marshall as teacher appears in "Lessons of Grace," a section comprised of lectures delivered primarily in classroom or workshop settings.

Her poems in "Rhymes of Grace," some of which are published with her tunes in hymnal collections, are not always serious, as "The Ode to Joe" makes clear, and the final portion of the book, "Tones of Grace," reflects further her light touch as she uses musical embellishments as take-off points for deeper observations about everyday life.

In *Grace, Noted* Jane combines old and new, simple and profound, tangible and intangible in such a way that one sees here a multi-talented, committed woman who has impacted the world of church music with far more than her well-known and much-loved choral compositions. Lay persons and musicians alike should find themselves both enriched and inspired as they read.

Natalie Sleeth

Publisher's Prologue

I wish I could claim the idea that produced this book; I cannot. That belongs to Rosemary Heffley, who suggested that Jane Marshall pull together the contents of *Grace, Noted*. I was interested to learn of the project, however, and equally pleased that we were selected as the publisher.

Our relationship with this delightful teacher/composer/editor/mother/alto in the Dallas Civic Chorus goes back 21 years. Still located in Chicago then, our company sponsored an Avery & Marsh workshop at Southern Methodist University in Dallas, and it was on that occasion that we first became acquainted.

Dallas in the early '70s was fertile ground for church music and church musicians. Along with Jane, composers Lloyd Pfautsch, Carlton Young, Natalie Sleeth, and Austin Lovelace were all a part of the community. It is no exaggeration to say that the texture of American choral music was significantly improved by the efforts of these talented people.

On a number of occasions, this entire group, including spouses, would get together to socialize and compare notes. I was privileged to be included in several of these gatherings and was even to host a dinner party for this group, when, unfortunately, my plane was forced down in Shreveport, Louisiana. Good sports that they were, they went ahead without me.

Several years later we asked Jane to serve as an editor with W. Thomas Smith, Austin Lovelace, and Carlton Young for *HYMNAL SUPPLEMENT II* (Agape © 1987). It was a pleasure to work with her in this capacity and to meet yet another side of this gracious person.

The Marshalls, Jane and Elbert, make a great team. When I first met Elby, he was working for Texas Instruments, but he always had a great interest in and love for the music of the church. It was clear that he was and still is involved in and supportive of Jane and her work.

As this book will document, Jane is an adept communicator. Having spent much of her life as a teacher, she knows how to create impelling word pictures to retell Bible stories, as well as stories of her own life and the lives of Christians with whom she has lived and learned. This ability also has given her the opportunity to write both hymn and anthem texts for much of the music she has written.

This book pulls together the various facets of her life. The total picture gives us the essence of Jane Marshall. She has been gracious enough to pool examples of her teaching days as well as new offerings never before published.

Church musicians will delight in Jane's writings and insider's perspective, but her collection of stories, lessons, rhymes, and tones of grace will be of value to all who seek to strengthen their Christian walk.

George H. Shorney

All the musicians who over the years have been participants in Church Music Summer School at Perkins School of Theology are the true parents of this book.
To them it is dedicated.

Table of Contents

I. Stories of Grace

	Page
The Outsiders	3
Seeds, Mystery, and Harvests	6
From Jerusalem to Georgia	9
Too Good to Be True?	14
The Clear Window	18
Uncomfortable Words	22
God, Caesar, and Artists	27
Can These Bones Live?	31
What Does It Take to See?	36
Two Gifts	40
Tu Es Petrus	44
Violence, Victory, and a Song	48
Bookends for Joy	52
Be Salty!	58
Paul and the Magician	63
Rise and Shine!	67
To the Mountain and Back	71
Chosen: A Symphony in Three Movements	74
A Lost 'Te Deum'	79

II. Lessons of Grace

Plastic Spoons or Sterling?	87
The Passionate Church Musician	90
Priests, Levites, and the Holy	95
Can the Director Teach It? Then Singers Can Sing It!	105
Tradition and Spontaneity	109
Teachers in the Church's Future	119

III. Rhymes of Grace

Has Anybody Seen Christmas?	125
Advent Prayer	126
Advent People	128
Will We Find a Way?	129
What Gift Can We Bring?	130
You Call Us, Lord	131
Ode to Joe	132

IV. Tones of Grace

Author's Note	135
Passing Tone	137
Neighbor Tone	139
Trill	141
Pedal Point	143
Appoggiatura	146
Escape Tone	148
Anticipation	150
Suspension	153
Grace Note	155

Stories of Grace

The Outsiders

(Published in Choristers Guild LETTERS, 1985. Used by permission.)

Matthew 2:1-12

In the time of King Herod, after Jesus was born in Bethlehem of Judea, wise men from the East came to Jerusalem, asking, "Where is the child who has been born king of the Jews? For we observed his star at its rising, and have come to pay him homage." When King Herod heard this, he was frightened, and all Jerusalem with him; and calling together all the chief priests and scribes of the people, he inquired of them where the Messiah was to be born. They told him, "In Bethlehem of Judea; for so it has been written by the prophet:

'And you, Bethlehem, in the land of Judah, are by no means least among the rulers of Judah; for from you shall come a ruler who is to shepherd my people Israel.'"

Then Herod secretly called for the wise men and learned from them the exact time when the star had appeared. Then he sent them to Bethlehem, saying, "Go and search diligently for the child; and when you have found him, bring me word so that I may also go and pay him homage." When they had heard the king, they set out; and there, ahead of them, went the star that they had seen at its rising, until it stopped over the place where the child was. When they saw that the star had stopped, they were overwhelmed with joy. On entering the house, they saw the child with Mary his mother; and they knelt down and paid him homage. Then, opening their treasure chests, they offered him gifts of gold, frankincense, and myrrh. And having been warned in a dream not to return to Herod, they left for their own country by another road.

If you're like me, you've heard the story of the three Wise Men so often your ears are almost vaccinated against it, and the familiar words go by almost voiceless, robbed of their power by frequent, if friendly, repetition.

Yet it's a wonderful story, once we overcome our immunity—a story that has as much to say to us—even us church musicians—as any story in the Scriptures.

In a scene in *The Lion in Winter*, King Henry looks out his window into the chilly night and says:

The sky is packed with stars.
What eyes the Wise Men had, to see a new one among so many!

What eyes indeed. Not everyone saw the star, certainly not the church folks, those scribes and Pharisees, who knew well the Old Testament prophecy. Yet these strange men from the East did see it, and, with the shepherds, were the only ones to come to the manger, worshiping and bringing gifts. Who were they?

They were not part of our crowd, but some of "those people." "From the East" in Bible language means "from a long way off," so we can translate Wise Men to mean witch doctors, gurus, astronomers, outsiders, Communists, goyim, half-way house inhabitants, obstinate pastors, even non-singing members of the children's choir—any group that is not part of our group. These people exist on the fringe, outside the comfortable and familiar confines of our own standards. It was to those outsiders, or Gentiles, the star appeared, and it was they who responded in faith to it, bringing their strange gifts and worshiping the tiny king who lay in a manger at the place where the star came to rest. Somehow they saw in the star a promise, so out of the darkness of their own lives they braved the desert and came searching for the one who could fill their need.

Surely there is darkness in our lives, too, in our homes, our churches, and on the front pages of our newspapers every day. Surely there are those outsiders in our lives, too—the ones who just don't seem to fit from time to time. What gifts do they bring? Even we feel like outsiders now and then. What gifts do we all bring to offer up at the altars of our hearts?

Surely one of those strange gifts is *need*. Those kids in our choirs who seem bent on destroying every rehearsal frequently are saying, "I need you!" so loudly we are deafened. Another strange gift is *threat*—threat to our perfection-worship sometimes. No one is more difficult to handle than the singer who can't sing on pitch but wants to be part of the group. I remember an adult, a graduate student at the seminary where I teach, who had this problem. The Seminary Singers themselves decided to see to it that that student remained in the choir; so all during that year, whenever the choir sang in concert, even at the annual Christmas Carol Service, that all-too-familiar sound of someone groping around in the octave below for the tune was painfully clear. Had I been the director, or a member of the choir, I'd have had a terrible problem, for my perfection ideal would have been severely jeopardized.

Fear can be a gift, too, that the outsiders in our lives bring forward. I can easily be the outsider here myself, serving as a church musician and now and then finding myself at odds with others on the church staff. Have you ever worked with colleagues like that, those so fearful of being overlooked or made to feel inferior they take control of every staff situation and impose their will even where it's not appropriate? Sometimes it takes the form, in pastors, of too much authority and inflexibility. Sometimes in church musicians it takes the form of insisting on a level of quality at the expense of someone's feelings. And sometimes pastors and musicians are fearful of each other simply because they occupy the same worship space on Sunday mornings, where everything is so very visible to so many people.

Need, threat, and fear—strange gifts.

That the Wise Men saw the star and came so far to find its promise was remarkable, but what they found when they arrived in Bethlehem was more remarkable still: a wrinkled, probably wet, crying baby in the lap of a 15-year-old unwed mother in a barn. Really! And yet they worshiped, betting their lives that this was indeed the fulfillment of the promise.

Epiphany is, next to Easter-Pentecost, the oldest festival in the Christian calendar, older by several centuries of observance than Christmas. And like the other great festivals, it tells what God has done, unlike our Rally Days and Laity Sundays, which celebrate what we have done. And it is truly marvelous in our eyes, so marvelous a piece of Good News that we can hardly believe it to be true. That God would come to outsiders, even unbelievers, on God's own, with no conditions or strings attached—what a Gospel!

And yet God does, again and again, inviting us to see that star and bet our lives on the promise. And God sets us in the midst of other outsiders who bring their gifts, presenting them as need, or threat, or fear, to our vulnerability, our humanness, and our own scarred selves, giving us Jesus, a cosmic model of unbounded love and acceptance, no matter how unmerited these are. The gift of the star pointing to the promise is our gift, too, and it lights up the desert and darkness before us today.

Seeds, Mystery, and Harvests

(Published in Choristers Guild LETTERS, March 1986. Used by permission.)

More and more I find the Gospel writers looking over my shoulder and reading my church musician's diary. Recently I realized Mark had done it again, and very directly, in his account of Jesus' descriptions of the kingdom of God.

"Kingdom" is a big word. It suggests immensity, majesty, and mystery, whether we encounter it in the Bible or recall its place in stories and legends we grew up with, those "kingdoms beyond the sea" that represented magical and marvelous realms our imaginations could enjoy. The "kingdom of God" referred to in the Old and New Testaments carries the same images but suggests an ethical dimension as well: the "yoke of the kingdom of God," an expression found in ancient Hebrew writings, charged the faithful Jew with responsibility for the creation and for life lived within it.

Mark in his Gospel does nothing to dispel the aura of mystery and immensity the phrase "kingdom of God" conveys but instead uses it to present us with a paradox, a favorite literary technique of many of the biblical authors.

Mark 4:26-32

And he said, "The kingdom of God is as if a farmer should scatter seed upon the ground, and should sleep and rise night and day, and the seed should sprout and grow, the farmer knows not how. The earth produces of itself, first the blade, then the ear, then the full grain in the ear. But when the grain is ripe, at once the farmer puts in the sickle, because the harvest has come."

And he said, "With what can we compare the kingdom of God, or what parable shall we use for it? It is like a grain of mustard seed, which when sown upon the ground, is the smallest of all seeds on the earth; yet when it is sown, it grows up and becomes the greatest of all shrubs, and puts forth large branches, so that the birds of the air can make nests in its shade."

Jesus here is trying to make clear what the grand concept of the kingdom of God is about to that motley collection of unlearned, unlikely fisherpeople who were his disciples. Surely the paradox must have seemed almost laughable to them, as indeed it does to us: God's kingdom on the one hand and as part of its flower this untrained, unwashed, unbelieving crew of followers, on the other. How in the world, each one of them must have thought, can I possibly be identified with such an enterprise as this? One can almost hear James or John saying, "Who, me?" as Jesus called them to the kingdom's work, or more likely still, "Who, them?" as they tried to envision their neighbors as part of the same vast plan. "Lord, are you kidding?" surely was in their minds if not actually on their lips.

Jesus, sensing their incredulity, then describes the kingdom to them in his parable of the farmer.

The farmer, his story makes clear, is just an ordinary farmer who gets up in the morning and goes to bed at night after doing the routine chores of planting, tilling the soil, watering, and weeding. There is nothing at all remarkable about him: he is not the Secretary of Judean Agriculture or professor of horticulture at Jerusalem University, only an ordinary farmer who does what ordinary farmers do, and he waits and watches and trusts that the seed he planted and nourished will in its own time produce. The seed, meanwhile, mysteriously takes root in the fertile ground and begins to grow. When the corn is ready, the farmer harvests it and enjoys it, perhaps sharing it with his neighbors. How it grows from minute seed to full-blown ears he does not understand; all this happens slowly and surely while he sleeps and eats and carries out his other routine duties on the farm. That the corn almost magically comes into full harvest occurs regardless of the education of the farmer or of his rank among his neighbors or of anything he does beyond that expected of any other farmer, and its yield is great in spite of its modest beginnings. In this regard the corn is not unlike the mustard seed, which grows to such great size it becomes a nesting place for the birds.

This is such a believable and homespun story I can relate to every part of it, yet at crucial times in my career as a church musician I seem to forget to do so. "Seek first the kingdom," Jesus has said. And my response so often has been either "Who, me?" or, as I look at the modest group of untrained singers in my charge, or the staff I must work with, or a church that borders on being downright indifferent, "Who, them?" Surely he must be kidding! The responsibility at times like that becomes overwhelming at most, laughable at the very least.

This is when Jesus, in Mark's account, talks directly to me, if only I will listen. Remember the farmer, he seems to say, as you choose music, move pianos, check attendance, exhort singers, raise budgets. He simply did his job and trusted God for the rest. He was not expected to do the impossible or the mysterious or anything else in God's jurisdiction. For he was not God. Sometimes, I must confess, when I seem to be more powerless than I want to be and need to feel I am more in control of things, I convince myself I have to be the world's greatest choir director—St. Cecilia herself—or Johann Sebastian Bach, or Margaret Hillis; and sometimes I even trespass on the territory that only God can occupy. For often my inadequacies for the task at hand become heavy burdens to bear, and my patience, unlike the farmer's, evaporates. I am so intent on achieving the goals I have set for my choir or my students or my music program (whose?) I forget to trust in that mysterious Power that makes seeds and music and musicians, and even non-musicians who sing in my choir, grow and flower and become blessings to those around them.

Jesus' reminder about the ordinary farmer simply doing his job—his only, no one else's—is a refreshing antidote for that heaviness of responsibility that often becomes the number one threat to church musicians as we measure our modest talents against the needs of God's kingdom. No wonder the "yoke of the kingdom of God" for those who have ears to hear is transformed by a new message:

*Take **his** yoke upon you and learn of him,*
*for **his** yoke is easy and **his** burden light.*

From Jerusalem to Georgia

(Preached with Patricia Evans at First United Methodist Church, Columbus, Texas, April 1991)

Acts 8:26-40

Once upon a time a young medical student named Philip Goodman enrolled in a highly regarded medical school in a city not far from here. One reason for the school's reputation was renowned faculty member Dr. Christopher Davidson, a pioneer in heart treatment and surgery, who, in addition to teaching, was doing research on heart transplant procedures and practicing medicine in the university hospital.

Though Phil had expected to enter the field of pediatrics, he was so inspired and fascinated by Dr. Davidson—his kind and caring manner, his commitment, and his remarkable skill as a doctor and teacher—that Phil began to draw away from pediatrics into coronary medicine. Dr. Davidson, perceiving Phil's interest and his character as well, called him into his office one day and asked him to join his small group of gifted students specializing in the treatment of heart disease. Phil immediately agreed, though he knew that Dr. Davidson's heart procedures were considered unorthodox and highly controversial by some and that therefore some risk was involved in the association.

During Phil's last year, Dr. Davidson was tragically killed, sending shock waves through the entire medical community and especially through the school and the young doctors who were his disciples. They finished their studies, though somewhat numbly, and continued into internship and residency.

Then the angel of the Lord said to Philip, "Get up and go toward the south to the road that goes down from Jerusalem to Gaza." (This is a wilderness road.) So he got up and went.

Phil, now with his medical degree, was in the process of searching for a practice to join, when one day the late Dr. Davidson's secretary called him to say, "We thought we had gone through Dr. Davidson's things and completely cleaned out his desk, but we just found a memo asking that I get in touch with you and tell you to go South before you settle down anywhere. 'Tell Phil to head for Waycross, Georgia,' it says, 'but on the back roads across the Gulf states, not Interstate 10.' That's all."

So Phil packed up his things, stuffed them into his ancient Toyota, and headed out the very next morning.

Now there was an Ethiopian eunuch, a court official of the Candace, queen of the Ethiopians, in charge of her entire treasury. He had come to Jerusalem to worship and was returning home: seated in his chariot, he was reading the prophet Isaiah.

Phil drove all that day and into the night, stopping finally at an all-night diner on a back road in Mississippi. Parked in front of the diner was one car, a very fine large car with a chauffeur in front and a very strange-looking man in back. Handsomely aristocratic, the black man wore beads around his neck, a ring in his ear, a hand-woven gown of bright colors, and jewelry on many of his fingers. He was reading a book. As Phil approached the car, he noticed it carried a diplomatic license plate from one of the islands in the West Indies. Trying not to stare, he made himself walk past the car into the diner.

"Who's the guy outside in the Lincoln?" Phil asked the counter man.

"Dunno, really," the man said. "Some sort of medicine man, looks like. His driver said he'd been over to the medical school for a seminar, but I couldn't find out much trying to talk to the guy himself. What English he knows, it sure don't sound like what we speak here in Mississippi. I gather, though, that he's some kind of bigwig government official, whatever country he comes from."

By this time Phil, consumed with curiosity, was sliding off the counter stool and making for the door to see if the car was still there. It was, with inside light still on and the strange man still reading.

Then the Spirit said to Philip, "Go over to this chariot and join it." So Philip ran up to it and heard him reading the prophet Isaiah. He asked, "Do you understand what you are reading?" He replied, "How can I unless someone guides me?" And he invited Philip to get in and sit beside him.

Phil hurried to the car and stuck his head into the open rear window. He was astounded to see the man trying valiantly to read aloud an old medical text on heart disease. "Do you know what you're reading, sir?" Phil asked. The strange man smiled and in very broken English answered, "How can I without somebody to help me? Would you be good enough to sit here beside me and explain it?"

The man was struggling to understand the author's prediction that with research moving so quickly, thanks particularly to a brilliant heart specialist, it would not be long before amazing heart surgery procedures would be perfected—bi-passes, new valves, even transplants—by which

10

thousands of heart disease victims could be radically cured.

The eunuch asked Philip, "About whom does the author say this, about himself or about someone else?" Then Philip began to speak, and starting with this scripture, he proclaimed to him the good news about Jesus.

Phil explained that his own beloved mentor, Dr. Davidson, had done the research the textbook predicted, lovingly and courageously taught it to his students, and used the methods to heal hundreds of patients who had come from all over the area to be treated. Phil told the man of the great doctor's death but assured him that the legacy he had left behind was his spirit, still alive and well, inspiring his followers, working through them, and continuing to make his presence felt.

As they were going along the road, they came to some water; and the eunuch said, "Look, here is water! What is to prevent me from being baptized?" He commanded the chariot to stop, and both of them, Philip and the eunuch, went down into the water, and Philip baptized him.

"I want to have this knowledge, too," the strange man said, barely able to contain himself, "and live and work in the spirit of your friend and teacher, Dr. Davidson. Is there anything to prevent that?" Phil took the man's hands in both of his and with tears in his own eyes, said, "Not a thing. You've learned what you need to know. Now all you have to do is trust it."

"Oh, I do, I do!" said the man.

When they came up out of the water, the Spirit of the Lord snatched Philip away; the eunuch saw him no more, and went on his way rejoicing. But Philip found himself at Azotus, and as he was passing through the region, he proclaimed the good news to all the towns until he came to Caesarea.

His new friend turned back to his reading, flipping pages of the book excitedly, apparently lost in his new-found knowledge. Phil suddenly realized that the big car was moving down the road away from the diner and his Toyota. When the car slowed at an intersection of two country roads, he quietly opened the door and slipped out without the man's knowing.

Phil walked back to the diner, climbed into the rickety Toyota, and resumed his journey toward Georgia. He found himself in one unheard-of town after another in the back country of Mississippi, Alabama, and south Georgia; in each town he talked to people at gas stations and general stores and cafes about medical care where they lived. Phil learned that no one had heard the revolutionary good news about heart transplants or other treatments introduced by Dr. Davidson. So Phil treated the sick people he found along the way, using the skills he had learned from his great teacher, even training some young people to assist him and inspiring many to become doctors so they could minister to their own neighbors.

* * * * * * * * *

As always, there are questions to ask about the stories in humanity's family album, as Dr. Victor Furnish calls the Bible. Certainly one of the first in regard to this particular story is, who are the principal characters here?

Some of them are our own selves, hidden behind the masks of Philip and the Ethiopian. One can nearly always find oneself in every biblical narrative as more than one of the characters, just as students of psychoanalysis have learned that they can be several characters simultaneously in their dreams.

Philip is definitely an important member of the cast: devoted, committed, able to listen, prepared to serve, and trusting of his revered Dr. Davidson. He's a man of action, too, ready to move when the command comes or opportunities present themselves.

The medicine man is obviously a man of intelligence and openness, greatly respected and highly placed in the government of his country. He is strange, however, belonging to another culture totally; peculiar in his dress and speech, even his color and other physical characteristics. But he is devout, and he is unquestionably serious about his inner life and work, having been to the great city to worship. He is eager to learn more about healing, and he is not afraid to ask for help.

The principal character, however, is that One who always is the "lead" in the many dramas that unfold in this album. It is Spirit of the Lord, of course, even though what we read and learn of that remarkable Reality is sometimes, though not always, revealed in what happens to other important characters in the stories. It is clear that this is a Spirit that is very active and caring, that is in charge, and that wants others to have the health and life abundant that Spirit offers.

A second question asks, what really is the message of this fascinating vignette? What it is *not*, certainly, is a plea for minority rights, important though that issue can be. No, what it spells out is that wonderful just-after-Easter word: first of all, that the Lord—that is, Love—is *alive*, even after that grisly crucifixion; and that he is present with us continually, caring about all of us—including those who seem strange, different, not of "our crowd"—and wanting us to follow God's way, shown forth since the day of creation through amazing, often unlikely, people and in God's own unbelievable works. It says something else, too: that the Lord works in many ways, some of them unexpected and often hard to understand at the time. Anyone who has had an insight into something not thought of before that leads to something good has very possibly been nudged by the Spirit. Other times the Spirit may emerge as curiosity, conscience, confrontation, sensitivity, or reason and common sense. One has to be listening and open to catch it, and frequently our antennae are not receiving. But this is a Lord who never gives up on us and who never lets us or events around us that seem tragic or hopeless be the last word about us.

An invitation then is offered after the questions have been addressed. The old preachers I remember from my Presbyterian childhood often called this "a call to decision." The invitation is for us to respond.

If this story is a guide, one response is to *listen* and be open. Another is to *trust* that Spirit, as Philip did, and as the Ethiopian did, too. And the last response is, of course, to act, to move, to *go*, as the key word and the unseen key character in the story direct us.

Result? *Life*—joyful and abundant, not an illusion of something either exciting or comfortably cozy all the time, but *real* life—even with all the in-spite-ofs. It is such good news that it seems too good to be true. And when the inexpressible needs expressing, we musicians like to join our other brothers and sisters who are artists and say it in ways that often mere words cannot adequately do. Who could sing it better than that unknown composer of the old black spiritual:

I'm gonna sing when the Spirit says sing!
I'm gonna move when the Spirit says move!
I'm gonna go when the Spirit says go!
And obey the Spirit of the Lord!

Too Good to Be True?

(Preached at Perkins Chapel, Southern Methodist University, Dallas, Texas, 1984)

Genesis 28:10-17

Jacob left Beer-sheba and went toward Haran. He came to a certain place and stayed there for the night, because the sun had set. Taking one of the stones of the place, he put it under his head and lay down in that place. And he dreamed that there was a ladder set up on the earth, the top of it reaching to heaven; and the angels of God were ascending and descending on it. And the Lord stood beside him and said, "I am the Lord, the God of Abraham your father and the God of Isaac; the land on which you lie I will give to you and to your offspring; and your offspring shall be like dust of the earth, and you shall spread abroad to the west and to the east and to the north and to the south; and all the families of the earth shall be blessed in you and in your offspring. Know that I am with you and will keep you wherever you go, and will bring you back to this land; for I will not leave you until I have done what I have promised you." Then Jacob woke from his sleep and said, "Surely the Lord is in this place—and I did not know it!" And he was afraid, and said, "How awesome is this place! This is none other than the house of God, and this is the gate of heaven."

When we first meet Jacob in this story, he is on the run. He has lied to and dishonored his father and cheated his older brother out of his inheritance. He has hidden behind the skirts of his mother, made a general mess of things, and now taken her advice to get out of town until this whole affair blows over and things cool off. So he sets out into the desert for his Uncle Laban's ranch.

Night approaches and, using a stone for a pillow, Jacob camps at an old Canaanite sanctuary, goes to sleep, and dreams of angels going up and down a ladder to and from heaven and of God saying to him, "I will bless you. I will bring you back to this land. I will never give up on you until I've accomplished my purpose"—the same promise God had given to Jacob's father and to his grandfather before him.

Jacob wakes up in a cold sweat, scared to death. "Surely the Lord was in this place and I didn't even know it," he says.

I'm sure Freud could have a good time with this story. I can't go into all that dream detail because I don't know how. But what I think we can hear for sure in the story is that Jacob is acknowledging the presence of God somehow in this desolate desert place, even though he hasn't been aware of it.

Another observation—and this is incredible to me—is his reaction to God's blessing. Not one ounce of joy is reported in that reaction or one ounce of gratitude. Yet this is an extravagant promise from God: "I will be with you wherever you go. I will bring you back home to this land. I will raise up a nation from you and your descendants, and I will not stop blessing you until I have accomplished my purpose." Could Jacob hear that?

Apparently not. But should it have been a total surprise? After all, the same promise had come to his father and his grandfather, to Isaac and to Abraham. Jacob was in line for it. Yet his response is not joy but fear. He utters not a word of thanks for the gift, though there is some acknowledgment of God's presence. Obviously he did not expect God to be there, for after all, the place was a pagan shrine. Do we have shrines where we don't expect God to show up in an unlikely way? I think of Texas Stadium and Reunion Arena in my Dallas area. How about some of our larger banks or our favorite restaurants? Our pagan shrines can be legion.

What was Jacob's problem? Whatever is the Genesis writer trying to tell us?

Surely it must be that Jacob, because of his fear, self-centeredness, and perhaps guilt, simply couldn't recognize God when God showed up and therefore could not receive the blessing. Now Jacob was a conniver. He had lied. He had cheated. If we read the whole story of his life, we see that, even though he made some changes (because God, indeed, never did give up on Jacob), that same thread of conniving, ruthless cunning and concern for *numero uno* characterizes his actions throughout. Aren't we all pretty much the same people throughout our lives? Though we make some changes in direction, we don't completely change our spots, do we? Yet God seems to accept us in spite of ourselves. Jacob cheats, lies, outwits, finagles; because he does, he mistrusts both God and those around him—which is to say he lives a life of self-centeredness and unfaithfulness. He is, as a result, a soul on the run.

No wonder the Old Testament lesson's Gospel twin for the week, Matthew 10:24-33, reports Jesus saying to his disciples, "Fear not. Don't be afraid of those that can kill the body, only of the kind of living that can kill body and soul."

We've heard Jacob's story. Does it have anything to do with us?

One time the late great Southern Baptist preacher, Carlisle Marney, preached a sermon at Perkins Ministers' Week that began, "There's a zoo in me." Now who of us cannot say at one time or another that he or she has not had a donkey, hyena, dove, lion, ostrich, eagle, or pig inside? I know I have—and still do at times. Could it be that we also have a little bit of Jacob in us? Not that we musicians and teachers are congenital textbook scoundrels. We perhaps don't live our lives as consistently conniving as Jacob did, at least at the beginning of his adulthood. However, is it possible that we can recognize the tendencies? I for one can very well remember discovering very early that I could make points with Mother if I invoked Daddy's name in the argument, because Mother hardly ever crossed Daddy and had great respect for his opinion. So I used him to buttress my arguments. As kids we learn pretty quickly how to play that game, though I usually lost.

And I must say (not that I like for you to hear this) that more than once I've been acutely aware of desperately stepping, if ever so lightly, on someone else unjustly if I were backed into a corner far enough and needed, I thought, to defend myself—mostly with words, at which I am pretty adept—but occasionally with actions.

Educators and church musicians are certainly not normally cheats or thieves; but, to use an almost simplistic example here, has any one of us not illegally photocopied music or teaching materials and managed to rationalize the action, even though, except under exceptional conditions, such photocopying is against copyright laws? Or is there anyone here working in a local church or school that has never taken advantage of the known weaknesses of another staff or faculty member, particularly if we feel that person is encroaching on our territory somehow?

But the Genesis writer is really trying to get at a deeper problem that Jacob struggled with all his life. The problem is evident in this short story of his nocturnal experience at Bethel. Jacob, as we say, could not receive. God came to him, not in judgment or disapproval, though goodness knows Jacob had it coming. God came in overwhelming grace, overlooking Jacob's obvious misdeeds, with this wonderfully extravagant blessing. Furthermore, that blessing had run in the family, and God had indeed been present all along; yet Jacob wasn't able to be open to God's knocking on his door. Jacob was not expecting it in that place. He lived his life without reference to this inability to receive, according to W.J.A. Power, Old Testament faculty colleague of mine. We see this over and over again as we read Jacob's story. "Surely the Lord was here, and I slept through it!"

Jacob couldn't trust anyone unless he set the conditions. He had to do it all on his own. Do you know folks like that—folks who seem to be uncomfortable when something is done *for* them and comfortable only when they are doing the giving or the planning? Have you ever worked for someone who simply has to be in control, sometimes in very subtle ways, so that you are not free to do your job without that person's insistent interference or manipulative changing of your plans and suggestions? No, we should not all be doormats and never leave a situation when it becomes impossible for us to do what we know to be our calling and our primary task. But sometimes we have to figure out ways to deal with difficult situations. Could it be that sometimes we might need to look in the mirror to see if, indeed, there is a little Jacob showing in us, too?

The story also says something about God's action here and the unbounded love and forgiveness with which God overlooked Jacob's insecurities and faults. Surely that says to us "go and do likewise" when we encounter those folks who seem to have such a hard time being comfortable when they're not in control.

We church musicians are not strangers to this kind of problem. Many of us know first-hand, for we *are* perhaps the problem. There is a flip side, sometimes, to the strong leader. The very thing which makes us good leaders stands in the way of our being good ministers. We like to be on the leading end—in charge, in control—and feel a bit uneasy when we are not in command. We believe that we can plan a good worship service. We have had good training and experience. But sometimes does it happen, that, if it doesn't go the way we planned, we feel that service fails, as if it were all dependent on us? Do we find it hard to trust anyone else in this area? Could there be a little Jacob showing here?

If Jacob had been open to the gift that was his, much hurt could have been avoided. We know that the fear and distrust that get in our way from time to time bring pain in the long run to ourselves and others. This is not God's doing. It is ours.

Now if that were the end of the story, we would go home sorrowful, surely, because Jacob's tale so far has been bad news. But that is not the end of the story. It never is in the Bible. Underneath all this revelation about us and about Jacob is the story of God. God kept God's promise all the way and did establish a nation from Jacob, just as God had pledged, in spite of Jacob's continual backsliding. I wish I could report that after the dream experience Jacob reformed totally and lived a converted life of generosity and trust. He did set up a monument on the dream site to commemorate the occasion, but he slipped back from time to time into his familiar pattern.

How good it is to have Jacob's story as a reminder of God's grace and love as we try to turn our lives in another direction.

The point of this story for me is that God's purposes and grace were far bigger than Jacob's obstacles to them. The blessing came anyway. It had, in fact, been present all along. Jacob was free to keep the door shut on his end as we are free, but that didn't stop God, who kept on knocking.

Jesus put it succinctly: "Behold I stand at the door and knock. Whenever anyone opens that door I will come in...."

Too good to be true? The Bible says, "No, it is not!"

The Clear Window

(Preached at Choristers Guild Mid-winter Workshop, Dallas, Texas, 1991)

Mark 1:4-11

John the baptizer appeared in the wilderness, proclaiming a baptism of repentance for the forgiveness of sins. And people from the whole Judean countryside and all the people of Jerusalem were going out to him, and were baptized by him in the river Jordan, confessing their sins. Now John was clothed with camel's hair, with a leather belt around his waist, and he ate locusts and wild honey. He proclaimed, "The one who is more powerful than I is coming after me; and I am not worthy to stoop down and untie the thong of his sandals. I have baptized you with water; but he will baptize you with the Holy Spirit."

In those days Jesus came from Nazareth of Galilee and was baptized by John in the Jordan. And just as he was coming up out of the water, he saw the heavens torn apart and the Spirit descending like a dove on him. And a voice came from heaven, "You are my son, the Beloved; with you I am well pleased."

Acts 19:1-7

While Apollos was in Corinth, Paul passed through the interior regions and came to Ephesus, where he found some disciples. He said to them, "Did you receive the Holy Spirit when you became believers?" They replied, "No, we have not even heard that there is a Holy Spirit." Then he said, "Into what then were you baptized?" They answered, "Into John's baptism." Paul said, "John baptized with the baptism of repentance, telling the people to believe in the one who was to come after him, that is, in Jesus." On hearing this, they were baptized in the name of the Lord Jesus. When Paul had laid his hands on them, the Holy Spirit came upon them, and they spoke in tongues and prophesied—altogether there were about twelve of them.

Ever since Adam and Eve, we believe that God has been trying to tell us how much God loves us and what that can mean for our lives and all of creation. But it is hard to know someone and to relate to someone that we've never seen. So God has been about the business of revealing

Godself through rainbows, through Sinai, through miraculous deliverance through Red Sea waters, through prophets' words, through still small voices. But somehow we mortals didn't get it, or we kept forgetting it, or we would get it wrong. So came the time when God must have said, "I'll just go down there myself." And so God did in the form of God's Son, a clear window through whom we could see Godself.

And here we are now in 1991 having come through another celebration of that Irrational Season (that's Madeleine L'Engle's term), when an unpredictable God in an unlikely barn through an unwed mother gave us the gift of an unbelievable baby—human flesh, an epiphany of Godself. And now after the day of Epiphany, which means revelation or manifestation, we are into the season when we read stories in our family album, the Bible, about God's continuing to reveal Godself through that Son. The album is full of snapshot stories beginning, of course, with the Wise Men, those outsiders who represented the whole world, not just the chosen folk, and now continuing with the record of Jesus' baptism, the first story of God's epiphany after the story of the Wise Men.

Then we have the Acts lesson, which goes along in the lectionary with the Gospel story of Jesus' baptism—a story about Paul and baptism itself.

What does that have to do with us? Perhaps the stories hold a hint. John baptizes, he says, with the water of repentance. He tells us that after him one is going to come who will do something far more wonderful. Somebody has said that the baptism of John, the baptism of repentance, is like a courtship, for in the Bible repentance means more than just being sorry. It literally means taking a new direction, turning around. It means making an active decision to go a different way. One remembers, for instance, those Wise Men, who returned from the manger by a different path.

Jesus goes to be baptized, not because he has need of repentance, but, as scholars suggest, because he wants to identify himself with humanity. Maybe it is to get confirmation that what he is feeling is to be his vocation and his destiny. You remember the voice of God itself says to Jesus, "You are my beloved Son," and something like a dove descends—a dove, which means more in the Bible than just gentleness and peace: it means creative power.

In the other story, which seems more like a Pentecost story than an Epiphany story, Paul encounters (this is after Jesus has come and gone) a dozen or so folks at Ephesus and engages them in conversation because they have become new believers. Paul says, "Did you receive the Holy Spirit when you became believers?" "No," they say, "we never heard of the Holy Spirit. We were baptized into John's baptism." Paul baptizes them in the name of Jesus and tells them that indeed Jesus is the one for whom John was preparing them.

Becoming aware, then, of that gift that was theirs, they were filled with the Spirit. They were very much elated, as the story says, and Paul, representing the community, confirmed the event with the laying on of hands, a ritual act which many of us still perform. How wonderful it is that the community surrounds us constantly with affirmation and confirmation of belief and faith and baptism.

What does this story, along with the Gospel lesson, say to us musicians? What's the difference between repentance and baptism into the Holy Spirit? I think the key word, the clue, is in that word *power*. First comes the preparation: you as church musicians have chosen that new direction and taken on the task of ministry. We prepare ourselves for something, we know not exactly what, far more wonderful than we've previously known. Then comes the Spirit—our relationship to Jesus and Jesus' life, death, and resurrection, God's clear window into what God's loving self is. Maybe realizing that, we can relate better to a God who always wants to create a loving eternal triangle, one with God at the apex, you on one corner, I on the other corner, and all of us connected. *Baptism into the Holy Spirit is becoming aware of creative power.* This is not our doing. It is God's gift, yet another version of that unbelievable gift in the barn when love came down at Christmas.

Imagine what it would be like to have the power to turn loose our fears, for instance—all our fears of our jobs, of our inadequacies, of other folks we have to deal with, of losing control.

Imagine what it would be like for us musicians to lose the fear of speaking up for what we know to be beautiful in our art and to demand that courage and commitment lovingly from the folks with whom we work.

Imagine what it would be like to have the power to turn loose of our guilt and dare to say *No* to some of those jobs that sap our strength, that keep us from doing our primary task well.

Imagine what it would be like to have the power to deal with the day-in-and-day-out, week-in-week-out drudgery that goes along with being a church musician, a children's choir director, a staff person—with the dullness, the paperwork, the phone calls.

Wouldn't it be good to have the power to turn loose some of our biases and relax a little bit? We could learn more about some styles that we haven't liked or didn't feel comfortable with, perhaps some of the hymnody that seems to mean so much to our congregations but not to us. Since all hymns are a part of our church-family history, maybe we need to learn more about them, include them, and know how to sing them in the style in which they were conceived.

Wouldn't it be wonderful to be free in the face of all these demands and opportunities? Being free may mean a lot of things. It may mean changing the situation. It may mean accepting it. It may mean resisting it. It may mean finding new interests, diluting the stress a little bit.

If I hear this story right, we have been baptized by virtue of Jesus' coming into that power. It's here in us. All we have to do is trust it. We have to "let go and let God," a cliche I always thought was almost too cute; like all cliches it is so true that we get vaccinated against the sound of it. However, it really *is t*rue. It is a gift, that creative power. Baptism into repentance is something we take an active part in, turning ourselves around so that we can be ready for a gift, which is baptism into the Holy Spirit, i.e., God's gift of creative power.

Love has come. Repentance has taken place (and takes place continually, again and again, in our lives). Then we become aware of the power which is right there inside us, and we begin to feel the strength, the joy, the release, the freedom to serve and to be alive and once again to be reminded that God is still at it—working at God's epiphany, revealing Godself in the love that is Christmas, in the power and promise of that Spirit that came afterward. In epiphany God lets us see through that clear window of Jesus' life, teaching, death, and resurrection, what God is like, how much God loves us, and how to complete that eternal, beautiful, loving triangle that helps us accept not only God's love, not only other people, but even helps us accept ourselves.

What an irrational season when Love came down. What an incredible baptism into fire and life through the gift of an unbelievable baby, God's clear window into God's loving self.

Do you dare, do I dare to believe it?

Taking that dare involves a risk, and that leap into the unknowable is precisely what faith is all about.

Uncomfortable Words

(Previously unpreached and unpublished)

Amos 5:18-24

*Alas for you who desire the day
   of the Lord!
Why do you want the day of
   the Lord?
It is darkness, not light;
   as if someone fled from a lion,
   and was met by a bear;
or went into the house and
   rested a hand against the
   wall,
and was bitten by a snake.
Is not the day of the Lord
   darkness, not light,
   and gloom with no brightness
   in it?
I hate, I despise your festivals,
   and I take no delight in your
   solemn assemblies.
Even though you offer me your
   burnt offerings and grain
   offerings,
   I will not accept them;
and the offerings of well-being
   of your fatted animals
I will not look upon.
Take away from me the noise of
   your songs;
   I will not listen to the melody
   of your harps.
But let justice roll down like
   waters,
   and righteousness like an
   everflowing stream.*

Matthew 25:1-13

"Then the kingdom of heaven will be like this. Ten bridesmaids took their lamps and went to meet the bridegroom. Five of them were foolish, and five were wise. When the foolish took their lamps, they took no oil with them; but the wise took flasks of oil with their lamps. As the bridegroom was delayed, all of them became drowsy and slept. But at midnight there was a shout, 'Look! Here is the bridegroom! Come out to meet him.' Then all those bridesmaids got up and trimmed their lamps. The foolish said to the wise, 'Give us some of your oil, for our lamps are going out.' But the wise replied, 'No! There will not be enough for you and for us; you had better go to the dealers and buy some for yourselves.' And while they went to buy it, the bridegroom came, and those who were ready went with him into the wedding banquet; and the door was shut. Later the other bridesmaids came also, saying, 'Lord, lord, open to us.' But he replied, 'Truly I tell you, I do not know you.' Keep awake therefore, for you know neither the day nor the hour."

Do you react as I do when you hear this lesson from Amos read? I want to put my hands over my ears. It makes me feel very uneasy and very uncomfortable, because I love not only music but liturgy. These words have threatened me. I decided it was time I dealt with them, because I suspect that when words from the Bible hit us this way they are really saying something we need to hear. I tried as best I could to listen and learn.

What I found out when I began to read about the background of the text was that in the eighth century B.C. the northern kingdom, i.e., Israel, was a very affluent society. Amos was not one of the elite, but a simple shepherd. He lived in the border country between the north and the south, however, close enough to know what was going on in the cities of the north, possibly by listening to travelers on trade routes through that very craggy, desolate, desert country.

In this wealthy culture the rich were getting richer. And because they were "blessed," God, they were certain, was smiling on them. Things were going well. Their relationship to Yahweh was cozy. God was their buddy. They had God in their hip-pocket—or so they thought.

Meanwhile, people across the tracks lived in abject poverty—scratching out a living, finding food from any trash they could get, such as crumbs thrown from the tables of the rich, who lived self-righteously in their enclave of affluence and complacency, while the poor suffered in the ghetto.

Amos observed all this and was called to speak out, even though he was not one of the establishment prophets; for an interesting feature of affluent culture in Israel was the privileged class' strict observance of ceremonial, of the Sabbath, of the feast days. The liturgy was rigorously honored and became another vehicle for the people's belief in their own righteousness before God and of God's being a smiling God on their side.

That was the state of affairs then. It is clear as we look at today's world that little has changed. Recognizing that in many ways we are in the same boat as those folks so many hundreds of years ago in Israel, we can draw conclusions about the message the story sends to us church musicians and liturgists.

We should make two general observations. What we first hear Amos saying to those temple-going folks is that God is not only a God of mercy and grace, but a God of justice and judgment. As a pastor friend loves to say, "Judgment and mercy should be thought of as one word. You should say them so fast they run together: Judgmentmercy, judgmentmercy!" There is no way in the biblical understanding to separate God's justice or judgment and God's mercy. Second, this passage says clearly that this judgment *will* come.

If you use the lectionary in your congregation, you know that this particular lesson from the Old Testament falls two weeks before Advent's arrival in the fall. It is a foretaste of one of Advent's messages: judgment. Certainly nobody likes to hear that. Yet what is it specifically saying to us?

We know that the twin lesson that goes along with this one in the readings for this particular Sunday is Matthew's story that Jesus tells about the ten bridesmaids, five of whom were foolish because they didn't keep their lamps trimmed and burning and weren't ready when the bridegroom came. The total message seems to be: 1) The God of judgmentmercy will come; 2) be ready, because you don't know when that is going to happen.

I also think about another word from Jesus when I hear these uncomfortable words from Amos. (We need not think that the Good News is confined only to the New Testament or a word of judgment is confined only to the Old Testament. The whole Bible is judgment and Gospel.) Remember the rich young ruler asking, "What must I do to be saved?" Jesus' answer was, "Go sell everything you have and give to the poor and follow me." Now, that's an extreme statement, as were those statements from Amos reporting from God: "Alas for you who desire the day of the Lord. Why do you want it? It is darkness and not light. I *hate* your festivals! I take no delight in your solemn assemblies. Take away from me the noise of your songs. I will not listen to the melody of your harps." That hurts.

So consider this: because God is a God of grace, judgment will come in order that all people may know that grace.

What that calls us to do, certainly, is to be *sensitive* to the needs of others. For musicians, liturgists, and teachers it is not saying, "Give up your vocation and go join a march of protest of some sort. Get into a cause; give up your music. Forget working on your beautiful liturgy." After all, does not beauty speak to the poor in spirit? Where does the care of *all* those who are poor fit into our concern, our musicianly, liturgical, educational concern?

Surely it says keep balanced; be empathetic; don't get so wrapped up in your ceremonial and your beautiful sound that you forget the God of justice, who loves everyone and who desires well-being and peace and justice and freedom and food for all God's children. Open your eyes and look around you!

Music belongs to everyone. I can not tell any of you reading these words how to go about the business of making yourselves aware or of making your choirs and your classes acutely aware of the poor and the oppressed. You have to find that out in your own way and do what you can in your situation as a musician. But grace-filled justice, indeed, *will* come, and we are expected to have something to do with it. Will we be part of the problem that prevents it or part of the solution that helps see it established?

Concrete evidence exists that indicates some musicians are very much aware of the poor and are trying to do something about them through their music. A large church in downtown Dallas, for instance, has a very fine outreach program of mission to inner city people. Every Saturday during the school year and on weekdays during the summer, children from the inner city are bused to the church, where teachers provide instruction, food, field trips, and recreational activities. In the summer of 1990 Choristers Guild, a national organization serving children and youth choir directors, got in touch with that church and said, "What would you think of our using our endowment fund to pay the salary of a teacher to come to teach music every day to those elementary school children?" The church was delighted, so a pilot program began whereby a musical organization, historically active in music programs in the local church, reached out and took its services into the inner city.

Not all of us can do that, but maybe there are other possibilities. I know of some youth choirs that take work trips rather than concert tours in the summer. They sing some, but they also help in underdeveloped areas to rebuild houses, to clean up neighborhoods, and to work with local churches to help their people and their youth improve living conditions.

Now lest you think I am trying to say we must always move out of our accustomed place of making music into the inner city or to under-privileged areas, let me hasten to add that music can be a powerful force, being beauty itself, wherever it is shared—in the church, in the concert-hall, in the classroom, on recordings at home. People who make music— teachers, composers, performers—are enablers and inspirers, because music, like love, becomes a verb when it is shared. What is required of us as musicians at the very least is to share music that is as beautiful as we can make it with as many as we can, remembering the poor in spirit as well as the poor in body. Even those who are privileged can be helped by music to move out and to become aware of the need all around them and to do something about it. When we inspire them with beautiful music, I think we are in some degree helping folks who are poor in body and spirit, too.

Be aware, be sensitive, be caring, this story says. Open your eyes and help your choirs open their eyes so that all of your music, your ceremonial, your feasts, and your Lord's days can be an offering of true sacrifice that will be pleasing because you have acted on not only the words of Amos: "Let justice roll down like waters and righteousness like an everflowing stream," but also those words from the prophet Micah: "With what shall I come before God? Burnt offerings? The fruit of my body for the sin of my soul? God has told you what is good. What does God require of you but to do justice, love mercy, and walk humbly with your God?"

These are uncomfortably wonderful words, always meant for our good because they are words of judgment within the context of mercy from a God who, first of all, is a God of love.

God, Caesar, and Artists

(Preached at First United Methodist Church, Georgetown, Texas, October 1990)

Matthew 22:15-22

Then the Pharisees went and plotted to entrap him in what he said, so they sent their disciples to him, along with the Herodians, saying, "Teacher, we know that you are sincere, and teach the way of God in accordance with truth, and show deference to no one; for you do not regard people with partiality. Tell us, then, what you think. Is it lawful to pay taxes to the emperor, or not?" But Jesus, aware of their malice, said, "Why are you putting me to the test, you hypocrites? Show me the coin used for the tax." And they brought him a denarius. Then he said to them, "Whose head is this, and whose title?" They answered, "The emperor's." Then he said to them, "Give therefore to the emperor the things that are the emperor's, and to God the things that are God's." When they heard this, they were amazed; and they left him and went away.

Thank you for inviting me today. I know that I, a Dallasite, am a stranger to most of you in Georgetown, Texas.

I think a tie binds us, however; and it is much stronger than any distance that separates us. That tie is the Word—the one that we spell with a capital letter; the one we experience in so many ways, as John Wesley reminded us, the one that we apprehend as well through our reason, through scripture, and through tradition. It is these latter two that I want to say a few things about today.

The gospel story that we heard is that familiar one in which the good Jewish lawkeepers of their day asked Jesus a question; and, indeed, it was a trap question. We know it so well: "Tell us, is it lawful to pay taxes to Caesar—the emperor—or not?" That is an either/or trap question, even if one's intentions are not all as bad as we think the lawkeepers' intentions may have been.

Jesus gives them the answer their question deserves. "Well, look at the coin. Whose picture is on it?" "Caesar's." "Then give to Caesar what is his and to God what is God's." Not a great deal of help, was it? Jesus knew how to provide responses that provoked the right question, or at least provoked some thinking. The question that naturally would follow, of course, is, "What is Caesar's, exactly?"

If you were like me thinking about this familiar passage of scripture, though perhaps not too deeply, you had an image of two equals—maybe two competitors—say, God and Caesar, on a level playing field with a 50-yard line in between, all the turf on one side of that 50-yard line belonging to Caesar, and all the turf on the other side belonging to God.

Thinking more deeply, we know better than that. The Pharisees, being lawkeepers, of all people, knew better than that. We know, I think, that the image would be better if it went something like this: God is an infinite sphere encompassing us, standing over and above us, watching over us, in whose arms we rest. Nothing exists beyond that sphere or circle because it is so large and all-encompassing. Inside it rotate all of our lesser allegiances: those to the state (Caesar); those even to our dear ones, our family and friends; those to the Church; those to the Bible, and those to every other loyalty, idea, person, or group that we can think of—most of which allegiances are good.

We know that God comes first, but I find that hard to remember all the time. I have to be constantly reminded. Sometimes I get my priorities messed up, my loyalties out of order. I can very easily put the nation, my family, my dear friends, my art, the Bible (for there is such a thing as bibliolatry) first. Putting these before God is just plain idolatry. We know this when we think deeply about that temptation.

We find it even harder to know how to make decisions among our various allegiances that will serve God first. Always we know that to be in grateful response is to be obedient to the commandments, the first of which is, "You shall have no other gods before me." We know that even when that priority is in place it is very difficult sometimes to decide the better of two goods.

For instance, I may have on my schedule a worship commission meeting or a liturgical arts task force meeting or a music committee meeting. Very important decisions have to be made at this particular church meeting. But someone in my family at home—a child or husband—for some reason also seems to need immediate attention. I consider both of these claims on me very worthy, important claims. How do I serve God best? Do I give up the church meeting and stay home, or do I go to the church meeting and leave what I consider to be a need unfulfilled at home?

We know that whenever we must choose between the better of two goods—and don't we have to do this again and again in one day?—one of those goods is going to go unfulfilled. We face situations daily that call for choices like this, where we want to serve God best but don't always know how. The fact of the matter is that we might make the decision to stay home one time and serve God best by leaving another time.

I want to suggest that the second part of these few words that I have to say has to do with YOU. YOU are the ones that help me decide. Not just you in a particular place right now, but the Community of which all of us count ourselves a part—that kind of a remnant Community that dares to call itself the People of God. Frankly, without that Community I can't keep myself on track. Without it I don't think we can hope to keep ourselves in order in such a way that we can really fulfill an important purpose for which we were put here: to serve the needs of a hungry world.

It's this Community—right here and in other church buildings—that normally meets to worship on the Sabbath that I want specifically to mention. It is YOU. It is the Community, gathering week after week, that reminds me of what I forget so often. God indeed is first, and that Community helps me, strengthens me, and supports me in making those difficult decisions which reflect that reality responsibly. That Community also forgives me when I make the wrong choices.

The psalm for today said, "God keeps faith forever." I am reminded of this most urgently when we read the psalm together. I doubt that I would pick it up and read it on my own. In fact, I very much doubt that I would come to church very regularly if I were all by myself. You see, for me it takes the Community and the memory of the Community past—that would include my father, my forebears, and all of those kinfolk we read about in the Old Testament, because we are a part of that crowd, too. I also count friends who I know march to the same drummer as part of the Community whether they attend church regularly or not.

Furthermore, I must confess this to you who are, I think, very much like me because so many of us are involved in music and the other arts. It is the art forms that you give to me on a Sunday morning by which I am reminded in an inexpressible way through music, through beautiful visuals, through dance, through poetry, through hymns, through stained glass and architecture and sculpture, that freight the Word to me. I need to see, hear, and sense it, over and over again, not only as a word of reminder, and perhaps judgment, to keep me on the track, but particularly as the Word of grace that is the last word when our words about ourselves and each other are not.

This is the Word that was in the beginning that forgives over and over, seventy times seven times seven hundred times seventy. That Word has been promising and giving ever since Day One by rainbows, by doves, by tablets from Sinai, by freedom from bondage through the Red Sea, through the Word made flesh—that supreme revelation that we celebrate not only on Christmas but on every Sunday, which is a little Easter—that Incarnation which shows us best that God is love and that even death is not the last word about us.

How many times have I sung the Gloria Patri when, frankly, my mind has been elsewhere? How many times have I sung the Doxology simply out of habit? Yet strangely, even when I've sung it out of habit, the Doxology has said something to me. I need to perform that ritual. I need to be reminded, regularly—not just with sermon and scripture read, though those are very important to me—but so very particularly through the art forms that other members of the Community prepare and offer. Do not underestimate the power art forms exert on us and on others who may not be trained in any of the arts but who receive them and react and respond to them in a way that sometimes words can not even do adequately. William Cowper's hymn says:

*Sometimes a light surprises
the Christian while he sings.*

Singing with you somehow I am better able to rejoice in the knowledge that God indeed is first, and that together we can dare to risk ourselves choosing between goods, knowing we forgive each other, as God forgives us, when we make wrong choices.

Can These Bones Live?

(Preached at Northaven United Methodist Church, Dallas, Texas, 1987)

John 11:1-45

Now a certain man was ill, Lazarus of Bethany, the village of Mary and her sister Martha. Mary was the one who annointed the Lord with perfume and wiped his feet with her hair; her brother Lazarus was ill. So the sisters sent a message to Jesus, "Lord, he whom you love is ill." But when Jesus heard it, he said, "This illness does not lead to death; rather it is for God's glory, so that the Son of God may be glorified through it." Accordingly, though Jesus loved Martha and her sister and Lazarus, after having heard that Lazarus was ill, he stayed two days longer in the place where he was.

Then after this he said to the disciples, "Let us go to Judea again." The disciples said to him, "Rabbi, the Jews were just now trying to stone you, and are you going there again?" Jesus answered, "Are there not twelve hours of daylight? Those who walk during the day do not stumble, because they see the light of this world. But those who walk at night stumble, because the light is not in them." After saying this, he told them, "Our friend Lazarus has fallen asleep, but I am going there to awaken him." The disciples said to him, "Lord, if he has fallen asleep, he will be all right." Jesus, however, had been speaking about his death, but they thought that he was referring merely to sleep. Then Jesus told them plainly, "Lazarus is dead. For your sake I am glad I was not there, so that you may believe. But let us go to him." Thomas, who was called the Twin, said to his fellow disciples, "Let us also go, that we may die with him."

When Jesus arrived, he found that Lazarus had already been in the tomb four days. Now Bethany was near Jerusalem, some two miles away, and many of the Jews had come to Martha and Mary to console them about their brother. When Martha heard that Jesus was coming, she went and met him, while Mary stayed at home. Martha said to Jesus, "Lord, if you had been here, my brother would not have died. But even now I know that God will give you whatever you ask of him." Jesus said to her, "Your brother will rise again." Martha said to him, "I know that he will rise again in the resurrection on the last day." Jesus said to her, "I am the resurrection and the life. Those who believe in me, even though they die, will live, and everyone who lives and believes in me will never die. Do you believe this?" She said to him, "Yes, Lord, I believe that you are the Messiah, the Son of God, the one coming into the world."

When she had said this, she went back and called her sister Mary, and told her privately, "The Teacher is here and is calling for you." And when she heard it, she got up quickly and went to him. Now Jesus had not yet come to the village, but was still at the place where Martha had met him. The Jews who were with her in the house, consoling her, saw Mary get up quickly and go out. They followed her because they thought that she was going to the tomb to weep there. When Mary came where Jesus was and saw him, she knelt at his feet and said to him, "Lord, if you had been here, my brother would not have died." When Jesus saw her weeping, and the Jews who came with her also weeping, he was greatly disturbed in spirit and deeply moved. He said, "Where have you laid him?" Jesus began to weep. So the Jews said, "See how he loved him!" But some of them said, "Could not he who opened the eyes of the blind man have kept this man from dying?"

Then Jesus, again greatly disturbed, came to the tomb. It was a cave, and a stone was lying against it. Jesus said, "Take away the stone." Martha, the sister of the dead man, said to him, "Lord, already there is a stench because he has been dead four days." Jesus said to her, "Did I not tell you that if you believed, you would see the glory of God?" So they took away the stone. And Jesus looked upward and said, "Father, I thank you for having heard me. I knew that you always hear me, but I have said this for the sake of the crowd standing here, so that they may believe that you sent me." When he had said this, he cried with a loud voice, "Lazarus, come out!" The dead man came out, his hands and feet bound with strips of cloth, and his face wrapped in a cloth. Jesus said to them, "Unbind him, and let him go."

Many of the Jews, therefore, who had come with Mary and had seen what Jesus did, believed in him.

The story of Jesus raising Lazarus from the dead is a fascinating one, as are most of the stories in the gospel of John, who is both cryptic and metaphorical. In this particular story John is almost like a first-century Alan Alda, who not only acts in but frequently writes and directs "Mash," that show of anti-war shows. In the midst of bloody operating room scenes, in the midst of gunfire, in the midst of absolute military hell in Korea is the story of peace. It is told, of course, with a wonderful light touch that, along with its poignancy, makes it an absolute winner.

So now here comes John with his story of Jesus as the revealer, as the light, as the fountain, as the good shepherd, as the bread—all images in John's gospel and in today's story, as life itself. John illustrates this by showing us, of all things, Death. And I mean Death with a capital "D." Death is all over the place.

There are five scenes in this little drama. Mary and Martha, Lazarus' sisters, send for Jesus because Lazarus is sick unto death. The disciples question the trip because they know if Jesus gets to Bethany he is getting into territory where he is likely to be apprehended. His time is about up. He has become a threat. He knows it. Even the disciples know it, and good old Thomas, whom we think of as the "doubter," says, "If he's going, let us go, too, and die with him." More than one death is being discussed here.

At Bethany, where the family lives and which has been like a home to Jesus, he encounters Martha and Mary. They visit the tomb. Jesus raises the now very dead Lazarus; mourners weep and wail. Death abounds, as it does in Ezekiel's vision of that field of dry bones, an old Testament story assigned by the lectionary to go with John's account.

In this tale there is a tomb, a gravestone, graveclothes, even the smell of death. There are mourners weeping and wailing, the grieving family, even Jesus' grief for Lazarus, who was a good friend. I suspect Jesus is thinking about his own end as well. He knows good and well it is coming and that he must set his face to Jerusalem, where death is waiting. Death is, after all, worth grieving about, for life is such a gift. Grief is truly an appropriate reaction when death abounds.

Do we not experience death these days? Certainly we do if we pick up the newspaper or listen to the evening news. Terrorism, violence, drugs, accidents, crimes, obituary notices, the death of businesses, savings and loans, banks, institutions, relationships, even of honor, run rampant through our society. We wonder, too, as God asks Ezekiel: "Can these bones live?"

Death comes in many guises, as John tries to tell us. What do we know about spiritual death? What does it mean to be dead? To have no feeling? To be unable to be sensitive to others? To be cold, without emotional warmth? What is it like not to grow or feel pain? (Sometimes those are synonymous.) What is it like to be closed, not willing to accept what is new or surprising or what is not in one's control? What is it like to feel hopeless or without a sense of humor? Surely there is more than one kind of death.

But, enter Jesus, and all of a sudden life walks into the scene. Martha says, "Lord, if you had just been here our brother would not have died." Jesus says, "Your brother will rise again." Her response is, "I know, Lord, at the resurrection, at the last day." But Jesus says, "*I* am the resurrection and the life." So in the midst of Martha's doubt life comes anyway. Yet Martha's doubts are not completely erased. She turns around after Jesus has suggested going to the tomb and says, "Oh, no! Lazarus has been dead four days. He smells." Her doubts linger on. Humankind knows something about that too, I expect.

God says to Ezekiel, "Can these bones live?" Ezekiel says, "God only knows." But Ezekiel obeys, and life is breathed into those dead bones. So there is a choice in the midst of faith and doubt. Some believe; some are skeptical. Some act, in spite of their doubt. Which will it be?

Life springs up in this story in the face of death. Have you seen life in the presence of spiritual death, as it sometimes springs up in the midst of illness, even, which suggests death? I have a friend who brings life into a room wherever she goes. She's just that way: I don't think she can help it. I had the measles when I was about nine. Charlotte had already had them, so she came by to see me one day after school. I was miserable. It was the sickest I had ever been as a child. I had a high fever. The room was dark. Charlotte came in and got me laughing as she always did, and when she left I was virtually on the way to recovery. I didn't feel sick anymore. Tell me about holistic medicine. Tell me about life in the midst of the smell of death, even measles!

My mother is in her 90s. Most of her contemporaries are gone. She lives in a nursing home. She is losing her hearing and sight. She is losing her ability to get around and requires a walker. But she hasn't lost her life! She is the liveliest person I know—much livelier in mid-90s than I am in mid-60s.

Many of us know people who have illnesses, who are sick unto death, who are living to the full one day at a time. (As if the rest of us could do anymore than that, actually.) In the midst of death there is life. Could it be that in the midst of institutions and of relationships that are at risk, in the midst of sick governments, there is life?

Another illness smelling of death is the increasing emphasis in the church on the numbers game: getting people into the church with activities that will simply attract people quickly, such as singing upbeat music that will appeal instantly to everybody. Nothing is said about quality, nothing is said about appropriateness or historical tradition; we are just asked to do whatever we must to get folks into church.

Could it be that, in the midst of the apparent death of fine arts, there is life? Phasing out fine arts in the public schools is a sickness. We have never needed the arts as we rationalists and technologists do now. The salary scale for those in teaching in the arts and in church music is dangerously anemic. Can these bones live? Can there be warmth and caring—caring enough to fight for what one believes about beauty and what it says to the spirit? Can there be life in the midst of apparent death, even though this kind of growing means pain? Can there be hope and joy in the midst of this bloody scene?

If I read this story correctly, life is present; every day we are called upon to make a decision about it and, like Ezekiel, to go ahead and act as if we believe life will win even in those times of doubt—to be about the business, even though we may be a minority, of making music and bringing beauty, art, and loveliness wherever we can into the world with the best kind of selections and performances possible. It takes a bit of trust, because it takes a willingness to risk.

I believe this story is partly about a miracle, but primarily about trust—trust that, even in the midst of doubt and death, life is being offered. The decision is whether to accept the offering or not, whether to trust that it is a gift. Presents may not come in the form we predict, but the tradition tells us life has always come and it promises to continue to come.

As a friend has said, "All I can do is accept this mystery of life; to savor it, to suffer it, and to celebrate it!"

Can these bones live?

To bet our lives that in God's hands we can learn the truth about life and say Yes is to experience life abundant.

What Does It Take to See?

(Previously unpreached and unpublished)

II Kings 2:4-14

My first brush with old Lige, the great prophet, the one who restored the worship of the one God to Israel, was by way of Felix Mendelssohn. When I was 10 or 11 years old and we went to prayer meeting every Wednesday night, my parents were wise enough to let me loose to go to choir practice in a neighboring room and sit in with the adult choir. Fifty years later I can't remember very much of what they rehearsed besides *Elijah* by Mendelssohn. I got a big dose of that, and I thought it was wonderful. What I vividly recall are "the fiery, fiery horses and the fiery, fiery chariots" and a lot of magic performed by a great prophet and memorialized in a great big fat book of music by Mendelssohn.

You've read the story. The great prophet, old Lige, is about to die and he knows it. Twice he has told his faithful deputy and disciple, Esh, (let's call them these names to keep from getting mixed up) to stay behind while the Lord takes him to where he has called him—to Jericho and then to the Jordan, which really means he's going to go away to die by himself. In spite of the warning of the establishment prophets—call them the National Guild of Hebrew Prophets—who say, "Don't you know he's going to die? Do what he says and don't go with him," Esh, the loyal deputy, replies, "No, sir. I am going with you, Lige." And he does.

Elijah doesn't die on the first two trips (one of these occurs in earlier readings), but the third time, which is included in our lection this particular Sunday, Lige says to Esh, "The Lord has called me to the Jordan. You stay behind." This time the National Guild of Prophets, who had been hovering close by on the two previous occasions, stood far back. Why? I'm not so sure. But what do the words "Jordan River" say to you? Remember the spiritual "Deep River"?—"Gonna cross over into campground"? Remember the River Jordan had very strong connotations to folks in those days. It seems to have stood for both death and life, perhaps new life in death.

At any rate, Lige says he is going to the Jordan, and again the Guild of Prophets says to Esh, "Don't go with him. Can't you see he wants to go off to die alone?" Again Esh says, "For God's sake, no, I'm not going to stay behind. Lige, I'll go with you!" And he does.

So as they walk toward the Jordan River, old Lige takes off his cloak or mantle or stole and rolls it up, striking the waters with it. The waters part. They walk across those deep rivers onto dry land on the other shore. As they resume their walking, old Lige says to Esh, "What do you want me to do for you before I'm taken up?" Esh replies, "Let me inherit your spirit." That's what the "double portion" means in the reading. This was simply the rightful share that the eldest son got, the inheritance he was due. "Let me inherit your spirit."

"Well," old Lige says in so many words, "that's a tall order; but I'll tell you what. If you see me when I am taken up, you'll get your wish. If you don't, you won't." Suddenly they are separated by a whirlwind. Old Lige disappears as chariots of fire and fiery horses appear. In a flash it's over, and there stands Esh, but not before he says, "My father, my father, the chariots of Israel and their horsemen!" In other words, "I see! I see!"

Now Esh stands alone. The vision or the experience has ended. Esh rends his clothes, then he picks up the mantle—the stole—of old Lige, goes back to the shore of the Jordan, and holds it. He strikes the water with it, just as old Lige did, and says, "Where is the Lord of Israel?" The waters part. Esh crosses back over those deep waters which have separated to leave dry land for him to walk on and resumes the work of the great old prophet, Elijah.

Though Elisha, the scholars tell us, and I think we can read it in the accounts that follow, was not as great a prophet as Elijah was, he carried on the work Elijah began and did it responsibly. That's the story then.

What's the story now? Is it, as I seemed to think when I was 10 or 11 years old (with some good reason), about whirlwinds and fiery horses and fiery chariots? When prophets were mentioned in the Bible, they were usually almost supernatural, very strange. They were set apart. That's how the Bible let us know how important and special they were. But is that all the story? If it isn't, what is, and what makes it *our* story? We know that this family album we have called the Bible is full of stories that are really not just the story of our ancestors, but our story, and primarily, God's story in relation to us all.

What does it take to see? That is the crucial question this story poses. "If you see me when I'm taken up, you'll get your wish that you will inherit my spirit." Seeing is essential.

I suppose the job description for Esh would have been identical to the job description for old Lige, the great prophet: industry, a passionate commitment to the God he served and to his vocation and to all those who shared in it; integrity, for certainly an honorable man he was; honor toward the people he served, but especially toward the God he served. Lige had these. Obviously, Esh had them, too, or he wouldn't have been such a committed, loyal deputy, beloved by old Lige.

But is that all it takes to see? I think nearly every person committed to a vocation fits a job description that includes industry, passionate dedication to one's Creator and to the vocation one has been called to, integrity, and even insight and inspiration. Surely those last two are part of it, too.

What it takes primarily, because not all of us have equal amounts of the above qualifications, is trust. I deliberately don't use the word faith, though it might be said to be synonymous. I'm afraid if I use it, it will suggest intellectual beliefs, and that's not what I'm talking about here; trusting with heart *and* mind is more to the point.

It took trust. And trust means risk. It means daring. It means wanting to see. It means relying on, truly, (here is where the belief comes in) God, vocation, and one's commitment to both. I think Esh had it just as the Wise Men had it. They did not know where they were going, but they were searching, and they trusted that star to lead them, those Gentile outsiders that weren't among chosen Jewish people. They went for miles and miles from far-off countries, following a star. To what? A manger, of all things. Certainly they didn't plan that. But they trusted.

We musicians have our prophets, heroes, and heroines, do we not? Bach. Robert Shaw. Nadia Boulanger. Speak of talent, commitment, passion, integrity, and insight incarnate! Helen Kemp. Gerre Hancock. Jean Bartle. The list could fill many pages.

Prophets are needed, and a present-day prophet doesn't have to be a weird kind of oddball; but prophets are absolutely necessary, and they occupy an important place in our community.

I think every one of you who aspires to be the best kind of musician, the best kind of minister, the best kind of music education person, the best kind of human being in your particular vocation has the industry, the passion, and the commitment. To be passionate means to be passionate about taking care of one's self, as well as taking care of others. It means being passionate about one's art, about all of our arts. And it means being passionate about the community we serve.

The great majority of church musicians have that. They have integrity and honor, they care about respect for the people they serve, the intention of the composers whose music they sing, the quality of the repertoire they choose. They have insight into themselves, so they can be self-critical, and insight into others, so they can be pastoral. Certainly they have insight into their art. They are perceptive.

But is there trust to leaven the mixture? Isn't that the first thing required? I have to be reminded of this again and again, because I try so often to do my job all by myself. I know I have to work hard and I know I have to study, but I don't always have the trust that I need, for I want to be in control so badly that I resist turning loose and accepting help.

Perhaps it will help to remember Esh's response to the gift. Once old Lige was gone, the first thing Esh did was to rend his clothes. That's the Bible's way of talking about humility. Surely most choir directors have had that feeling. "Who am I to be up in front of this choir?" "Why did I say I would take the children's choir when I haven't been trained adequately for it?" "How can I possibly do this job?" "I'm not up to it." These are the questions most often asked by the vast majority.

One remembers Moses trying to avoid God's call. Feelings of inadequacy came flooding in. According to this story, that mood of humility may not be a bad place to start. When one is humble and feels inadequate with industry and commitment, one can keep on learning. There are unlimited opportunities in workshops, schools, reading, listening to recordings, going to concerts. One never stops that. Humility seemed to be the first response to the gift of that spirit that Esh wanted to inherit, and humility opens the way for us.

But after Esh rent his clothes, he picked up the mantle, went down to the shores of that deep river, and took a risk. Nothing happened until he said (testing his power now), "Where is the God of Israel?"

So, once again, where do musicians get what it takes to risk their powers? Again, from trust: by calling on the power that is already theirs. The Spirit given in baptism is present all the time. It was promised by the Lord himself, just as God promised Noah with a rainbow, promised Abraham, Isaac, and even old conniving Jacob that Presence would never forsake them—that God would continue to bless them, in spite of themselves. So God continues to bless us and be with us. The power is already within us. All we have to do is trust it. And if we have the trust and humility to know that, we don't have to be geniuses, prodigies, or saints. We don't even have to be old Lige or old Lige's counterpart, Esh. But we can be ourselves and carry on the work responsibly, faithfully, and joyfully.

Two Gifts

(Preached at Northaven United Methodist Church, Dallas, Texas, 1990)

Exodus 20:1-17

Then God spoke all these words:
I am the Lord your God, who brought you out of the land of Egypt, out of the house of slavery; you shall have no other gods before me.
You shall not make for yourself an idol, whether in the form of anything that is in heaven above, or that is on the earth beneath, or that is in the water under the earth.
You shall not make wrongful use of the name of the Lord your God, for the Lord will not acquit anyone who misuses his name.
Remember the sabbath day, and keep it holy.
Honor your father and your mother, so that your days may be long in the land that the Lord your God is giving you.
You shall not murder.
You shall not commit adultery.
You shall not steal.
You shall not bear false witness against your neighbor.
You shall not covet your neighbor's house; you shall not covet your neighbor's wife, or male or female slave, or ox, or donkey, or anything that belongs to your neighbor.

Matthew 18:21-35

Then Peter came and said to him, "Lord, if another member of the church sins against me, how often should I forgive? As many as seven times?" Jesus said to him, "Not seven times, but, I tell you, seventy-seven times."
"For this reason the kingdom of heaven may be compared to a king who wished to settle accounts with his slaves. When he began the reckoning, one who owed him ten thousand talents was brought to him; and, as he could not pay, his lord ordered him to be sold, together with his wife and children and all his possessions, and payment to be made. So the slave fell on his knees before him, saying, 'Have patience with me, and I will pay you everything.' And out of pity for him, the lord of that slave released him and forgave him the debt. But that same slave, as he went out, came

upon one of his fellow slaves who owed him a hundred denarii, and seizing him by the throat, he said, 'Pay what you owe.' Then his fellow slave fell down and pleaded with him, 'Have patience with me, and I will pay you.' But he refused; then he went and threw him into prison until he would pay the debt. When his fellow slaves saw what had happened, they were greatly distressed, and they went and reported to their lord all that had taken place. Then his lord summoned him and said to him, 'You wicked slave! I forgave you all that debt because you pleaded with me. Should you not have had mercy on your fellow slave, as I had mercy on you?' And in anger his lord handed him over to be tortured until he would pay his entire debt. So my heavenly Father will also do to every one of you, if you do not forgive your brother or sister from your heart."

It seems to me that today's Old Testament and Gospel lessons can't be separated; they speak as one voice, especially to us church musicians. The first lesson is the familiar Ten Commandments.

Then we have the gospel lesson from Matthew's version about the king who forgave a great debt and his subject who failed to turn around and forgive his own debtors.

I want to paraphrase a spiritual, with apologies to whoever wrote that wonderful old song "Ezekiel Saw the Wheel." Suppose it went like this:

*...a wheel in a wheel way in the middle of the air.
The big wheel run by love
and the little wheel run by the Great Commands.
A wheel in a wheel, way in the middle of the air.*

That's exactly what the lessons tell us today.

I used to think of the Ten Commandments as bad news. We had to memorize them when we were in the Junior Department. That's all we had to do: memorize them. We didn't really have to learn much theology or interpretation about them. Junior Department age is the time to memorize things, it seems to me. Mrs. Cherry was very insistent that one of the first things we did every Sunday morning was to recite the Ten Commandments, the 23rd Psalm, the 100th Psalm, the Beatitudes, the Great Commission, and the Corinthians passage about faith, hope, and love. I'm ever so glad we had to do that, even though to us kids at the time it seemed a bother.

My feeling about the Ten Commandments at that time was that they were basically undesirable. There were so many things one couldn't do! Indeed, I think our society looks on laws today pretty much the same way. Thank goodness we have them; however, we all seem to be of the opinion at one time or another that they are designed to hurt or restrict us. We are so adversarial now that as a society we are at each other continually in lawsuits. And we like to compete with each other, whether we're driving a car or playing in a contest of some sort. We want no restrictions.

I never even thought in those early days—and sometimes I don't remember now—that there was a preamble to the Ten Commandments just as there is a preamble to the U.S. Constitution. If you're like me, you can't recite the Constitution, but I'll bet you had to memorize the preamble.

The preamble to the Ten Commandments is very short, and we treat it even less significantly:

I am the Lord your God who brought you out of Egypt, who brought you out of slavery.

The preamble of the Constitution is similar:

We, the people...in order to establish justice, secure the blessing of liberty for ourselves and our posterity and to promote the general welfare....

Surely, then, both of these documents are gifts, just the opposite of bad news. And the only response that is really called for is the response of gratitude, which translates into obedience. In the case of the Ten Commandments, we obey by serving God and the neighbor. In fact, we know that when we do one we do the other. Similarly, the response to the Constitution is obedience to the law, which is really our expression of gratitude for it.

The Ten Commandments were always intended to be, as I understand it now, not specific rules, but broad guidelines. There are differences between rules and guidelines, or rules and principles. Since we musicians are now talking among ourselves, let me suggest that we could formulate some rules which are specific to our particular vocation, but which, if observed, fulfill the larger purpose of honoring the principles of the Ten Commandments.

For instance, as conductors of choirs or as organists, consider these:
—*you shall have no other goals before you as musicians in serving God than beautiful sound, carefully prepared and performed*
—*you shall not make graven images, i.e., perform cheap imitations of good music*
—*you shall not take your art in vain, i.e., irreverently, thoughtlessly, or lightly*
—*you shall remember quality and keep it holy*
—*honor your choristers, your composers, your art, and what these mean*
—*do not be unfaithful to them*

—do not kill them with either permissiveness or unkindness or neglect
—do not steal (by photocopying, particularly!)
—do not be envious of another's choir, organ, or congregation. There is a gift to be found, sometimes with great difficulty, in your own.

If the Ten Commandments were all we had in these lessons, they would make a strong point in themselves. The Great Commands, I think the scripture lesson suggests, are the "little wheel inside the big wheel."

"The big wheel run by love" is primary. Paired with the Exodus passage is the story from Matthew about the king who forgives the debt. He settles the accounts of his subject—suppose his name is Tom—who who has an enormous debt piled up. Tom has borrowed heavily from the king he serves. He owes some 15 years' wages, if you reckon that one talent was equal to about $1,000. In other words, Tom owes the king an impossible debt. Tom can't pay it, so he has to be sold. That was the way the king settled accounts and forgave debts, by releasing that servant from his service. But Tom begs for mercy and repents; though it's an impossible debt Tom can never repay, the king forgives.

Now Tom calls his friend Dick to account because Dick owes him 100 denarii. One denarius equaled about 20 cents. That's a manageable debt, not very big compared to what Tom owes the king. But what does Tom do? He does not forgive the debt. He slaps Dick into jail, unforgiving. Of course somebody tattles. The king gets word, and he peels Tom's skin and sends him to be punished severely. What this means in biblical language is not that God is going to "peel our skins," strip us, and throw us into jail or into hell. It simply is the Bible's way of saying this is a very serious matter. We reap what we sow. Sometimes others reap what we sow.

Tom was punished, then, not for the debt he owed the king, which was very large, but for not forgiving his debtor as Tom had been forgiven by the king. This is a story about forgiveness, the "Big Wheel." "The little wheel runs by the Great Commands, and the big wheel runs by love."

We have two gifts here. We have a gift of the law, and we can derive our own musician's rules and other rules and policies from that law. If we serve those rules, we can serve the larger principles and guidelines, which indeed are God-given.

We also have the gift of love prefaced by the word that we should love and forgive as we have been loved and forgiven. Is there a choir director among us who does not know how important it is to remember to be forgiving...of choristers, of congregations, of organists (the same things could be said of organists needing to be forgiving of directors), of pastors, and other staff members?

These gifts of law and love are reminders, veritable showers of blessing.

Tu Es Petrus

(Previously unpreached and unpublished)

Matthew 16:13-20

Now when Jesus came into the district of Caesarea Philippi, he asked his disciples, "Who do people say that the Son of Man is?" And they said, "Some say John the Baptist, but others Elijah, and still others Jeremiah or one of the prophets." He said to them, "But who do you say that I am?" Simon Peter answered, "You are the Messiah, the son of the living God." And Jesus answered him, "Blessed are you, Simon, son of Jonah! For flesh and blood has not revealed this to you but my Father in heaven. And I tell you, you are Peter, and on this rock I will build my church, and the gates of Hades will not prevail against it. I will give you the keys of the kingdom of heaven, and whatever you bind on earth will be bound in heaven, and whatever you loose on earth will be loosed in heaven." Then he sternly ordered the disciples not to tell anyone that he was the Messiah.

Recently a childhood friend visited me. We took a sentimental journey to downtown Dallas in the car so she could see how the city had grown and changed in 60 years. As we approached the intersection of Ross and Harwood, she looked at the office building on the southeast corner and asked, "Wasn't there a church there once?" "Yes," I said. "Mine."

What had happened was that my church had self-destructed, destroyed itself from within. After months of struggle and debate and unhappiness and fruitless attempts on the part of many to reconcile opposing opinions about doctrine and practice, presbytery found the only solution was to dissolve that congregation totally. Some buyer finally razed the building.

As I recalled that day, I thought of many of my music director friends today who tell me of the anguish and stress they are feeling because of holy wars occurring in the churches they serve. We see this in larger settings now, too, and the acrimony crosses denominational lines, from Southern Baptist to United Methodist to Episcopalian and Roman Catholic to countless others. In some congregations I know there are movements toward splits, pull-outs, dissolution. And this kind of thing is centuries old.

Suddenly a familiar biblical phrase pops into my head. While one voice of a two-part counterpoint sings its haunting, "Wasn't there a church there once?" the other—comprised of a choir made up of St. Matthew, Maurice Durufle, and Hans Leo Hassler, to name a few—intones that magnificent phrase of Jesus: *"Tu es Petrus"* or "You are Peter, and on this rock I will build my church; and the gates of hell will not prevail against it."

How to resolve the dissonant contradiction: my church that disappeared off that corner and the one Jesus promised hell could not prevail against?

We surely know that the church with the small "c" and the Church with the capital are not synonymous, but that the former is a part of the latter, hopefully a healthy part not requiring treatment or surgery, one that works in harmony to fulfill the mission of the whole Body. It is tempting at times to forget these two are not identical and see either the local church as too large and powerful or the Church Universal as too small, narrow, or weak—a trap not unlike the one J.B. Phillips wrote about in regard to our concept of God (Phillips, J.B., *Your God Is Too Small*; Macmillan, 1953).

We know also in our more thoughtful moments what this Church is not: just a location, edifice, particular dogma, ritual, or set of monetary, attendance, or other institutional requirements. But it is very hard to define exactly what it is, as a concept at least. Indeed, seeing the Church as a concept may be a mistake. For it is a "who," not a "what:" or, more precisely, a Community of "whos."

Then could it be that Jesus and Peter as they are pictured in Matthew's account can help us, as members and musicians in local churches and as part of that reality we call the Church as well, with a definition, and where we fit into it, especially under stress?

As I looked again at the "You are Peter" story in Matthew 16, I began remembering many of those other vignettes involving Peter, probably the most fascinating and transparent of all the disciples; and his profile sharpened with each descriptive adjective suggested in the accounts:

—impulsive, ready to speak first and think later; passionate, extravagant, never lukewarm; unable to keep his feelings a secret, as when at the Transfiguration he excitedly proposed building monuments to the three extraordinary figures in the vision, Moses, Elijah, and Jesus;

—hot-tempered, even violent under fire, as when he cut off the ear of the high priest's servant;

—humble, saying to Jesus on one occasion, "Go away from me, Lord, for I am a sinful man!"

—devoted, promising Jesus, "I will never leave you"; yet

—fearful enough to deny Jesus when the chips were down:

—trusting enough to risk walking on water to come to Jesus and to profess immediately on being asked by Jesus, "Who do you say that I am?" his intense conviction, "The Messiah of God!"

A mixed bag of qualities, for sure.

And this is "the rock?"

The Lord apparently thought so, which points to some of those adjectives clearly descriptive of that remarkable Self revealed in the Gospel, a Jesus who was also:

—devoted; especially drawn to Peter, along with James and John, who formed the inner circle of the disciples; but to others also, weeping with Mary and Martha at the death of Lazarus; and saying, "Greater love has no one than this, that one lay down one's life for one's friends";

—forgiving, accepting of Peter, regardless of Peter's obvious shortcomings, including three attempts at denial;

—perceptive of Peter's potential, and trusting of that to the point of declaring, "You are Peter, the rock on whom I will build my Church."

Having looked at such descriptions of both Jesus and Peter, it's important, I think, to make another observation about the "You are Peter" phrase; namely, that Jesus, though he declares Peter to be the material, the stuff, of which his Community will be built, is the One who will do the building, not Peter. In fact, one has to read past the Gospels into the book of Acts and into Peter's own epistles to discover more about these two amazing characters and what their stories mean. For after the resurrection a different Peter appears. The Builder himself, with Peter's trust in him, has turned the impulsive man of action into a man of aggressive decisiveness; the fearful, vacillating man into a man of courage and conviction, able to communicate persuasively—as on the Day of Pentecost—to people of varying backgrounds and understandings; a man still devoted to him but now to one ready and able to translate that devotion into ministry to others.

That was the Lord's doing, to paraphrase the psalmist, and it should be marvelous in our eyes.

For is not Peter all of us?

And are not those qualities perceived by Jesus as the raw materials of leadership in Peter ours also, if we can trust God to do the molding, building and supporting? Choir directors ministering to their particular music-making flocks, whether they be at peace with each other or in dissent, can know in the midst of their own moments of fatigue and questioning that they do not have to shoulder the whole load themselves and that the Church abides still, "in spite of dungeon, fire, sword," and whatever other agonies and diseases their local congregations are prey to. Pain and anguish, yes. But that has never been the last word for those who trust it is not.

Who are all the "whos" that comprise the Community in our day? One could never make an exhaustive list, but surely they include the scattered committed ones as well as the gathered ones—those who are, in many ways and places, going about the business of caring. Some, like many of you, are working with beauty, through all of the arts. Some are healing, sometimes with technical skills, sometimes with acts of kindness and thoughtfulness. Some are working for changes in the political and economic arena to better the lives of those in need. Some are teaching. Some are rearing families and tending to the elderly or to the planet itself and life upon it. Wherever there are those caring folks who translate their caring into action for the nurturing and enrichment of any part of the creation, trusting that not Evil but Love is the last word about that creation, there is the Church, as the words of "Ubi Caritas" (Latin Office Hymn, trans. by Richard Proulx, 1975; © 1975, G.I.A. Publications, Inc.) tell us:

Where true love and charity are found,
God himself is there.

I should mention that my own local church of long ago—the one my friend discovered had disappeared from that corner downtown—didn't totally vanish. The members dispersed into other congregations, one group scattering to various churches, thriving and more in tune with their particular needs, the other merging with a smaller congregation to form a congregation still alive and well in Dallas. While the church changed its configuration, the people of God, the Church, remained. So it has been throughout Judeo-Christian history, through fair weather and foul. And in each period of history and in each generation there have sprung up those leaders—ordinary folks with both rough and smooth edges to them, like Peter of old, who in trust have let themselves be sculpted into a Church by the Craftsman who promised hell should not prevail against that structure, remnant though it has always been.

"Peter—the 'rock?'" we ask, astounded.

"WE—the 'rock?'" we stammer, even more amazed.

Yes, we are told, again and again, and never more eloquently than by the old Rock himself in his first epistle:

"Like living stones," he says, "let yourselves be built into a glorious house, to be a holy priesthood,"

remembering always that Christ,

"the stone the builders rejected, has become the very head of the corner."

Violence, Victory, and a Song

(Previously unpreached and unpublished)

*The stars fought from heaven,
from their courses they fought against Sisera.*
—Judges 5:20

I am writing this during a week in which we are both celebrating the life and non-violent teaching of Martin Luther King and fighting one of the most devastating wars we have known in the Middle East. Both of these events coming at the same time have pushed me back to a strange story that for a long time I didn't even know existed because it's hidden in the fourth chapter of the book of Judges, a section of the Bible with which I don't normally have day-to-day conversation. I knew only about the song that follows it in chapter five, a song celebrating the events recounted in chapter four. How typical of a musician to remember the songs, but not always to know the details of the events about which they are written! (That observation tells us, I think, something about the power of the musical art form, particularly those of us who are church musicians—the power of our hymnody especially.)

To summarize the story:

The tribes of Israel in these early days of their history have only one common denominator, for they are very loosely connected politically. This is of course their belief in Yahweh, the one God. They are ruled by a series of judges, meaning, literally, "deliverers." Deborah is the judge here, and she happens to be a prophetess as well, dealing with the Israelites, who are again and again forgetting their God's commands and getting themselves into trouble, this time becoming enslaved by their enemies, the Canaanites.

When the story opens, they are under the heel of Jabin, a Canaanite king, and have suffered oppression, because of their backsliding, for 20 years. Deborah is ready to put a stop to the oppression, so calls in her chief-of-staff, Barak, saying to him, "Gather 10,000 strong men from the tribes and take them up to Mt. Tabor. The Lord will deliver the Canaanites into your hand." Barak has his doubts about the enterprise but agrees, provided Deborah goes with him. "I'll be right there," she assures him.

So Barak gets from the tribes of Naphtali and Zebulun the 10,000 good men and true and with Deborah leads them up the mountain. Now the Canaanite army, under General Sisera, is camped below in the valley of the Kishon River, where they have ready hundreds of iron chariots—tank divisions poised to obliterate any foe. The Lord, however, sends rain in torrents, the valley is flooded, the chariots are mired in the mud, and the Hebrew guerilla army swoops down from the mountain and totally exterminates Sisera's troops—every last man except for Sisera himself, who seeing (probably from the rear) that destruction is imminent, takes off running to escape capture or death.

His flight brings him huffing, puffing, and exhausted to the tent of Heber, a Hebrew clansman who has made friends with the enemy but is away from the tent, leaving only wife Jael to observe the approaching Sisera, now virtually on his last legs from the long run. "Come in, my lord, come in," Jael says, ushering Sisera into the tent.

"Hide me," he begs, "and tell anyone who comes looking for me you never heard of me."

Jael quickly covers him with a rug. Sisera asks for a drink of water and is brought milk instead. He promptly goes to sleep, whereupon Jael finds a tent peg and with a mallet nails it into Sisera's head with such force the peg passes through his head into the ground.

General Barak arrives at the tent searching for his enemy and is met cordially by Jael, who brings him into the tent and presents him with the dead Sisera.

Now where in the Bible is there a more grisly story than this?

The following chapter in Judges, then, contains the anthem in praise of Deborah, Jael, Barak, and the brave troops who wiped out the Canaanite forces, mentioning with disapproval the tribes who declined to participate in the battle. The arresting line in the song is the one quoted at the beginning:

> *The stars fought from heaven,*
> *from their courses they fought against Sisera.*

A violent, bloody battle, a ruthless murder, victory, and a song giving thanks for the victory. But victory over what? We need to probe further to find the answer.

Professor Richard Murray has suggested that Bible stories raise at least three questions that need addressing: What do they say about God? What do they say about humanity? And what do they say about the relationship between the two? (*Teaching the Bible to Adults and Youth*, Richard Murray, Abingdon Press, 1987) Seeing ourselves here may be the easiest of all, for we are at present in the midst of all this carnage in the Middle East that is forcing uncomfortable self-searching on us. And we are doing this even as we extol and give thanks for the work and life of Dr. King and his doctrine of non-violence, watching and listening to, almost nightly, hundreds of Americans singing, "We shall overcome," while both an American president and Saddam Hussein assure their people they are in the right—in Bible language, doing the will of God—just as Deborah and the Canaanite king believed about their own actions. And even we church musicians, who are about as far removed vocationally from war as any group could be, are called as citizens and as human beings to wrestle with answers for the tragic situation.

How do we *know* that we're doing the will of God?

My pastor friend Bourdon Smith shared some insights into this problem with me recently. He reminded me that Diettrich Bonhoeffer has told us in *The Cost of Discipleship* that to do the will of God nearly always guarantees we will be advocating change—proposing solutions that go against the ways of the culture and collide with the opinion of the majority in "a hostile environment" (Diettrich Bonhoeffer, *The Cost of Discipleship*, Macmillan Paperbacks Edition, 1963). The way of the Cross that we espouse more than likely will be difficult and unpopular.

A further measure of our doing the will of God is our capacity to love, not romantically or sentimentally, but inclusively; that is, to care about both friend and enemy and the planet we inhabit together as well, and to do so with humility, seeing into ourselves clearly enough to make certain pride is not the fuel that propels us into action.

And what does the story say about God and our relationship to that reality? Surely that God is on the side of the oppressed, in whatever century or circumstance they live. The song in the fifth chapter of Judges was one of thanks for victory over oppression, even though the thought patterns of those primitive people saw the deliverance in terms of gruesome military success. The witness of the biblical writers from Genesis to Revelation is not that God rejoices in killing people but in seeing them liberated from oppression, and the witness of Martin Luther King is that this is to be done non-violently, with Dr. King's added observation that oppressors are the most rigidly oppressed of all. When the "stars in their courses fought against Sisera," they were saying that oppression didn't have a chance; that freedom, like desegregation, was, as Senator Everett Dirksen put it during our civil rights struggle, an "idea whose time had come." This is clear; though in regard to method, today's world situation would suggest that we have reason to wonder how far we have progressed from the mind-set of violence to an understanding of non-violent doctrine of Dr. King and of Ghandi—indeed, of Jesus himself.

The God who hates oppression in any form is a God of love—pure, unbounded, and self-giving—who works through unusual people and events such as Jacob, Peter, a Baby in a manger, crucifixion, a resurrection to reveal love. And it is that love that is the conqueror in the end and that love we are called to respond to and reflect.

So songs of praise, the specific contribution and passion of musicians and artists, are very much in order, you poets, organists, singers, ringers, and dancers. They are appropriate, even in these violent days, while God is working God's purpose out. Joyfully make your beautiful art, music, and dance. With a voice of singing, declare ye this, in a song like the one those Israelites sang in the days of Deborah, when even the stars in their courses fought against Sisera:

> *Utter it even unto the ends of the earth:*
> *the Lord hath delivered his people. Alleluia!*

Bookends for Joy

(Preached at Northaven United Methodist Church, Dallas, Texas, 1987)

Acts 2

When the day of Pentecost had come, they were all together in one place. And suddenly from heaven there came a sound like the rush of a violent wind, and it filled the entire house where they were sitting. Divided tongues, as of fire, appeared among them, and a tongue rested on each of them. All of them were filled with the Holy Spirit and began to speak in other languages, as the Spirit gave them ability.

Now there were devout Jews from every nation under heaven living in Jerusalem. And at this sound the crowd gathered and was bewildered, because each one heard them speaking in the native language of each. Amazed and astonished, they asked, "Are not all these who are speaking Galileans? And how is it that we hear, each of us, in our own native language? Parthians, Medes, Elamites, and residents of Mesopotamia, Judea and Cappadocia, Pontus and Asia, Phrygia and Pamphylia, Egypt and the parts of Libya belonging to Cyrene, and visitors from Rome, both Jews and proselytes, Cretans, and Arabs—in our own languages we hear them speaking about God's deeds of power." All were amazed and perplexed, saying to one another, "What does this mean?" But others sneered and said, "They are filled with new wine."

But Peter, standing with the eleven, raised his voice and addressed them, "Men of Judea and all who live in Jerusalem, let this be known to you, and listen to what I say. Indeed, these are not drunk, as you suppose, for it is only nine o'clock in the morning. No, this is what was spoken through the prophet Joel:

> *'In the last days it will be, God declares,*
> *that I will pour out my Spirit upon all flesh,*
> *and your sons and your daughters shall prophesy,*
> *and your young men shall see visions,*
> *and your old men shall dream dreams.*

> *Even upon my slaves, both men and women,*
> *in those days I will pour out my Spirit;*
> *and they shall prophesy.*
> *And I will show portents in the heaven above*
> *and signs on the earth below;*
> *blood, fire, and smoky mist.*
> *The sun shall be turned to darkness*
> *and the moon to blood,*
> *before the coming of the Lord's great and glorious day.*
> *Then everyone who calls on the name of the Lord shall be saved.'*

"You that are Israelites, listen to what I have to say: Jesus of Nazareth, a man attested to you by God with deeds of power, wonders, and signs that God did through him among you, as you yourselves know—this man, handed over to you according to the definite plan and foreknowledge of God, you crucified and killed by the hands of those outside the law. But God raised him up, having freed him from death, because it was impossible for him to be held in its power. For David says concerning him,

> *'I saw the Lord always before me,*
> *for he is at my right hand so that I will not be shaken;*
> *therefore my heart was glad, and my tongue rejoiced;*
> *moreover my flesh will live in hope.*
> *For you will not abandon my soul to Hades,*
> *or let your Holy One experience corruption.*
> *You have made known to me the ways of life;*
> *you will make me full of gladness with your presence.'*

"Fellow Israelites, I may say to you confidently of our ancestor David that he both died and was buried, and his tomb is with us to this day. Since he was a prophet, he knew that God had sworn with an oath to him that he would put one of his descendants on his throne. Foreseeing this, David spoke of the resurrection of the Messiah, saying,

> *'He was not abandoned to Hades,*
> *nor did his flesh experience corruption.'*

This Jesus God raised up, and of that all of us are witnesses. Being therefore exalted at the right hand of God, and having received from the Father the promise of the Holy Spirit, he has poured out this that you both see and hear. For David did not ascend into the heavens, but he himself says,

> *'The Lord said to my Lord,*
> *"Sit at my right hand*
> *until I make your enemies your*
> *footstool."'*

"Therefore let the entire house of Israel know with certainty that God has made him both Lord and Messiah, this Jesus whom you crucified."

Now when they heard this, they were cut to the heart and said to Peter and to the other apostles, "Brothers, what should we do?" Peter said to them, "Repent, and be baptized every one of you in the name of Jesus Christ so that your sins may be forgiven; and you will receive the gift of the Holy Spirit. For the promise is for you, for your children, and for all who are far away, everyone whom the Lord our God calls to him." And he testified with many other arguments and exhorted them, saying, "Save yourselves from this corrupt generation." So those who welcomed his message were baptized, and that day about three thousand persons were added. They devoted themselves to the apostles' teaching and fellowship, to the breaking of bread and the prayers.

Awe came upon everyone, because many wonders and signs were being done by the apostles. All who believed were together and had all things in common; they would sell their possessions and goods and distribute the proceeds to all, as any had need. Day by day, as they spent much time together in the temple, they broke bread at home and ate their food with glad and generous hearts, praising God and having the goodwill of all the people. And day by day the Lord added to their number those who were being saved.

I have two bookends that a friend gave to me a long time ago. They are alike in weight and design. Standing between the bookends are volumes whose contents have changed the world. The bookends are a reminder to me of Easter and Pentecost, framing the amazing "great 50 days" in the Christian story.

At Easter the message was, "God—Love—is alive! Not even death or evil or anything else in all creation can put it down." But it was revealed to just a few here and there. The responses were varied: bewilderment, skepticism, or belief.

Something began to happen to the disciples during that 50-day period between Easter and what we now call the day of Pentecost.

Our Acts 2 story is full of amazing events: mighty winds, tongues of fire, people speaking in languages not their own. I don't intend to explain that. I can't. And I don't think that's the main point anyway.

What we do know is that it was an extraordinary time.

Pentecost tells us that "God is alive," but the thrust is to the whole community, not just to a few. The phrase, "Jews from every nation," is the Bible's way of saying, "Folks from all over the world—everybody." And these folks seemed to be all gathered together. That says something, doesn't it?

The theme here is similar to the theme expressed in the Epiphany story of the Wise Men, who represented the whole world, not just people who were thought of as the chosen ones. This was a story about inclusiveness.

Powerful love revealed at Pentecost in this strange way communicates to everyone, not just to the "insiders." But it does communicate! On this Mothers Day I like to think it communicates like a mother, whose love and voice and touch and feeding we know are essential to a baby's wholeness. Here is not just a verbal communication, though that is present also. There are other ways of communicating this close relationship of love and concern.

What does this say to musicians and people who work in the arts? Surely that the arts can express the inexpressible when words are simply inadequate. If the Pentecost story with the wind and the fire doesn't tell us that, I don't know what does. Drama was definitely communicating something there.

One of my favorite extended masterworks is the Brahms *Requiem*. Perhaps it's yours, too. Do you know that low "D" that occurs in the double bass part in one of those movements covers 18 pages of the full score? It goes on and on and on underneath all the other instruments and the chorus, which is singing at that time, "The souls of the righteous are in the hand of God." One doesn't have to be a musician to get the idea here of repose, of grace, of care and concern, and of closeness. No matter what language the *Requiem* is being sung in, Brahms indicates musically the strong supporting, loving hand of God with the low "D" that continues for so many pages.

Bach's cantata, "God's Time Is Best" [No. 106 written for Bach's uncle's funeral] is another musical work that conveys joy, faith, and assurance—in a way that words alone cannot express. If one simply listens to the music, one needs no sermon or eulogy.

Our own hymnals speak powerfully to large numbers of people. Some hear the message on some pages, and some hear it on others. If you don't know how powerfully hymns can convey feelings, you haven't talked to the hymnal committees that put these books together!

Powerful love or power-filled love, like that conveyed at Pentecost, can indeed change people and whole systems. The Spirit-power given to such a vast crowd of witnesses was something new, the thrust of Pentecost. Peter turned 180 degrees around from the time Jesus was alive to this particular Day of Pentecost. Something transforming happened to him and those other apostles as well.

My father did a 180-degree turn in his life, too. He was a boy from a small East Texas town, where, in the very early days of this century, a white person simply did not call a black person "Mr." or "Mrs." and did not shake hands with a black person. But I very well remember my father's example of always addressing a black person as "Mrs." or "Mr.," and we were introduced that way and we shook hands. Whether it was my mother's love or whether it was my father's preacher-father's wonderful life and teaching coming to fruition in him, I don't know; but something happened. He had a "Great 50 Days" experience somewhere in his life and spent much of his adult life in social work dealing with all kinds of folks as brothers and sisters.

Need we be reminded of the difference the church, in its better moments, (regardless of how we feel about its bureaucracy) has made in the world? What it is doing in Central America, for instance? What it is doing in the Soviet Union? The church is a force to be contended with regardless of skepticism and doubt and error. The church continues to speak out against oppression and exclusivity in the face of popular opinion, though often that voice represents the minority, "the remnant."

I think a word of caution is in order here to those of us who work in music—composers, performers, teachers. We talk here about Pentecost as the spreading of a worldwide movement, as something with an emphasis on community. We know that individuals cannot always make as much difference as groups in effecting social change. But this is not necessarily a call for us musicians to band into unions or collectives or to abandon what we do and to join a Peace Corps or a cause, though we are called to be aware of these movements and make some difference in our own way. It seems to me that the word of caution is, don't think you have to abandon your vocation and join a great movement. As Luther would say, "If you're a shepherd, *keep on* being a shepherd!" If you're a musician, keep on being a musician! The world needs you and your art more than ever. Don't disdain your calling because it deals primarily with beauty, not social justice.

One time I asked the late hymnologist-theologian, Erik Routley, "What about all the old gospel songs that we know that stress 'I' instead of 'We'? Are we now to avoid these?" "Oh my, no! Of course not," he said. "When we all sing them together, they become 'WE,' don't they?" So when we do our jobs well—with faithfulness, with study, with trust—something happens not all of our doing, and the effect is the effect that we make together.

I think we can forget about being competitive, though, and work together wherever we can in our art. There is something powerful about the community that Pentecost gave birth to that is adding a new dimension. The whole world is included in this wonderful Good News. We need to respond together in spirit.

A United Methodist clergyman, Bishop Wheatley, told the story of a young pastor in Yuma, Arizona, who during the great blizzard of 1983 got a call from a farm family who was missing a little daughter who had not yet gotten home from school. The pastor got 50 people together and began a search in the blizzard for the child. They searched unsuccessfully until they were numb with the cold. Finally someone said, "Let's join hands and make one last sweep across that field that she has to cross to get from school to home." They did it. Sure enough, somebody stumbled on a bush under which they discovered the dead body of the little girl. The father was in the group and, as he picked the child up to carry her body home, he cried, "Why, in God's name, didn't we join hands sooner?"

Even though we do our jobs singly, we are part of a community, and that community, whether we always feel this is so or not, is filled with powerful love. Our response to that is, as always, a decision. Will we risk our pride, fear, doubts, and image to trust that power-filled love? Will we reach out to work in a kind of community with other musicians, whether we know them or not, to do what is beautiful? That can be powerful. Will we risk it? Will we dare? Even in our times of doubt, will we *act* as if we believe?

Be Salty!

(Preached in Perkins Chapel, Southern Methodist University, 1989)

Mark 9:38-50

John said to him, "Teacher, we saw someone casting out demons in your name, and we tried to stop him, because he was not following us." But Jesus said, "Do not stop him; for no one who does a deed of power in my name will be able soon afterward to speak evil of me. Whoever is not against us is for us. For truly I will tell you, whoever gives you a cup of water to drink because you bear the name of Christ will by no means lose the reward.

"If any of you put a stumbling block before one of these little ones who believe in me, it would be better for you if a great millstone were hung around your neck and you were thrown into the sea. If your hand causes you to stumble, cut it off; it is better for you to enter life maimed than to have two hands and to go to hell, to the unquenchable fire. And if your foot causes you to stumble, cut it off; it is better for you to enter life lame than to have two feet and to be thrown into hell. And if your eye causes you to stumble, tear it out; it is better for you to enter the kingdom of God with one eye than to have two eyes and to be thrown into hell, where their worm never dies, and the fire is never quenched.

Job 42:1-6

Then Job answered the Lord:
   I know that you can do all
      things,
and that no purpose of yours can
      be thwarted.
'Who is this that hides counsel
      without knowledge?'
Therefore I have uttered what I did
      not understand,
   things too wonderful for me,
      which I did not know.
'Hear, and I will speak;
   I will question you, and you

declare to me.'
I had heard of you by the hearing of the ear,
but now my eye sees you;
therefore I despise myself,
and repent in dust and ashes."

The story provoking the title of this little talk begins with the disciples following the Rabbi around near Capernaum and John saying to the Rabbi, "There's another man over here healing folks with power. We've tried to stop him because he wasn't following in our group." And Jesus says, virtually, "But he *was healing* folks." And then follows that famous quote: "Whoever is not against us is for us."

That set me to thinking about salt, for Jesus goes on, as you have read in the lesson itself, to conclude with the comment about being salty. In the encyclopedia I discovered that salt had at least 14,000 uses. It's used in making glass, paper, soap, rayon, leather, and roads, to name just a few. And as we all know, it's still used to preserve, to season, and to purify. How many times has your doctor told you to forget those over-the-counter gargles and use hot salt water when you have a sore throat?

Old Job himself somewhere in his poetry says, "Can an unsavory thing be eaten that's not savored with salt?" I know how many times I've tried to cover up my cooking with a little too much seasoning, particularly salt. And I found out that the Hebrews used to rub their newborn babies with salt. The Arabs would say, "There is salt between us" meaning "We have eaten together and we are therefore friends," as we would say of a communion service or seder. Caesar's legions were paid in salt; hence the word in English, salary, and the phrase, "So-and-so's not worth his salt."

The Rabbi says, have salt in yourselves; in other words, be salty. What can this mean for us? What did it mean in the first century? Obviously, as the story goes on, the first requirement of those disciples after they had complained about some outsider doing good was to accept those not in their group who ministered anyway. For us these could be workers outside our institution or organization, the professional, for instance, versus the non-professional. You can translate professional any way you want, either someone who is formally trained or someone who is paid, and a non-professional as either an untrained person or a volunteer. All good music enriches humanity. To be salty means to accept those musicians making good music outside the church as well as in it.

Surely the Good Samaritan was one of these so-called outsiders, as was Rabbi Lefkowitz. My mother, who was a staunch Presbyterian all her life, loved Rabbi David Lefkowitz who was the rabbi of our Dallas

Temple Emanu-El many years ago. I can remember Mother saying, "In so many ways he is more Christian than a lot of us." He didn't belong to "our crowd," but he was lovingly doing the work that we stand for and believe we are called to do.

Jesus, the Rabbi, said, "Accept the others that are not in our group," and, as a corollary to that, "Be caring of those little ones," meaning be caring of those who are beginning their journey. They may be folks who are on a musical pilgrimage or folks who are on a faith pilgrimage. But Jesus' word was to be caring and accepting of them. And then his language got a little stronger. In essence he said, "Don't you dare put a stumbling block in their way that would prevent them from moving forward toward maturity on their journey." You'll see Jesus had even harsher words than that if you read the story word for word. The strong language is simply the Bible's way of indicating that this is a very serious matter—that we, in doing these things wrongly, reap what we sow.

Then he talked about the disciples themselves. He said in paraphrase, "Discipline yourself, therefore. If there is a part of you that is a stumbling block to yourself and to your community or to those little ones, cut that part off so that it doesn't poison the whole body. You're better off being healthy without that one arm or leg, so to speak, than you would be if you had that diseased part of you infecting the whole body." Discipline yourselves. Repent, that is, do not simply be sorry, but turn around, take a new direction. That's what Jesus is saying when he says, "Cut it off; purify with salt that part of you that seems to be a stumbling block."

How do we identify our particular stumbling blocks? I think of competition, for one thing. I see myself falling into the trap of being a competitor in almost everything I do—even in the way I drive my car—to be the first off the block when the light turns green. But as a musician particularly I see it in myself as a composer and in some of my friends who are composers, though I'm sure we are unaware of this at the time. There was an occasion in which I participated that I never have forgotten, even though I still fall into similar traps. Some of us composers were together at a party one night when we got into the business of material published, publishers, what publishers we had heard from, royalties, and so forth; and it got to be a game of one-upmanship—not in so many words, but that's what was happening. First one would tell a story about his or her publishers, and then someone would come up with one that was just a little bit better or more complimentary. It was really rather fascinating to watch—and embarrassing.

What of our schools, our music departments, our voice studios, our organ studios, our organ workshops? What of our church choirs, our church staffs? Do you see competition for various church members to be part of your class or your choir which might prevent them from being part of another class or group that meets at the same time? Competition can be a stumbling block.

Competition's corollary is arrogance. It may be undiscovered by many of us. I see it, for instance, in regard to those folks who have DMAs and those folks who may have no degree at all, at least not a doctorate. The DMAs may not want to be arrogant, but is there a little feeling of superiority there? This can occur on either side: it's very possible for those who don't have a doctorate to feel superior to those who do. That's reverse arrogance, reverse discrimination. DMAs may be thought to be not quite in our humble crowd.

It shows up sometimes in the choice of music. I see an arrogance on the part of some choir directors, some favoring one style and some favoring another and each feeling arrogant about his or hers—which means that those other people just don't quite come up to them in some way and are not in their group. What all choirs need in their repertoire is a balance of all styles, the use of the best of all styles so all kinds of folks can be served—those who like the music of the Renaissance and some for whom the gospel hymn says a great deal—whether either one of those styles is a director's particular choice or not. Here's where being salty means to season and be at peace with each other.

Then in comes old Job, jumping out of the Old Testament and acknowledging, after his long, dramatic, poetic presentation, his arrogance, his own stumbling block, as if he could know the ways of God. When he did acknowledge and realize that indeed he had tried to know the ways of God, he repented and expressed it very vividly: "I had heard of you by the hearing of the ear." In other words, "I'd heard of Noah and the rainbow of promise from God. I'd heard of God's saving his people by bringing them across dry land, parting those Red Sea waters, pulling them away from Pharaoh and out of bondage into a land of promise." He'd heard of old Jacob, the conniver, at Bethel finally saying, "Surely the Lord was in this place and I didn't even know it." And God was saying to Jacob all along, "I will never leave you until I've accomplished my purpose in you. I will bless you, bless you, bless you and your children and your children's children." Even old Jacob! So, when Job said, "I'd heard you with the hearing of the ear, but now that I have repented and turned around and realized what my stumbling blocks to myself and others have been, my eye sees you." Which meant that God is God, God is good, and God is love.

That says to me that when I risk turning loose, accepting others, and cutting off that part of me—that competitiveness, that arrogance that destroys not only my community and the people I want to serve (the neighbor, in other words), but my own self—when I can risk that, then I think I can hear what Jacob heard in that blessing. That's a gospel that's not confined to the New Testament. It runs all the way, as my mother would say, "from A-to-Izzard"—in our story, from Genesis to Revelation.

And that blessing in language dear to us musicians, particularly those of us who work with hymn books or old American folk melodies, says,

> *That soul, though all hell should endeavor to shake,*
> *"I'll never," says God,*
> *"No, never forsake."*

Paul and the Magician

(Preached in Perkins Chapel, Southern Methodist University, 1989)

Acts 13:1-12

Now in the church at Antioch there were prophets and teachers: Barnabas, Simeon who was called Niger, Lucius of Cyrene, Manaen, a member of the court of Herod the ruler, and Saul. While they were worshiping the Lord and fasting, the Holy Spirit, said, "Set apart for me Barnabas and Saul for the work to which I have called them." Then after fasting and praying they laid their hands on them and sent them off.

So, being sent out by the Holy Spirit, they went down to Seleucia; and from there they sailed to Cyprus. When they arrived at Salamis, they proclaimed the word of God in the synagogues of the Jews. And they had John also to assist them. When they had gone through the whole island as far as Paphos, they met a certain magician, a Jewish false prophet, named Bar-Jesus. He was with the proconsul, Sergius Paulus, an intelligent man, who summoned Barnabas and Saul and wanted to hear the word of God. But the magician Elymas (for that is the translation of his name) opposed them and tried to turn the proconsul away from the faith. But Saul, also known as Paul, filled with the Holy Spirit, looked intently at him and said, "You son of the devil, you enemy of all righteousness, full of all deceit and villainy, will you not stop making crooked the straight paths of the Lord? And now listen—the hand of the Lord is against you, and you will be blind for a while, unable to see the sun." Immediately mist and darkness came over him, and he went about groping for someone to lead him by the hand. When the proconsul saw what had happened, he believed, for he was astonished at the teaching about the Lord.

The story in the daily lectionary for this day seems to be a very straight-forward one. It's like a first-century morality play, an early church "Gunsmoke," where the forces of good represented by Paul and the forces of evil represented by Simon Bar-Jesus shoot it out in the square of one of the cities of Cyprus.

Now why did the church include this particular story in the canon? Does it have anything in the world to say to us today?

The first thing I had to ask myself when I read this strange but fascinating story was, "What are magicians anyway?" Surely, they are folks who deal in illusion. Most of the magicians we like to think about are the ones that entertain us, the ones that are fun. These are not the ones, of course, that the story is talking about.

The magicians the story refers to, represented by Simon, are trafficking in illusion; they are bending the truth for their own gain. Sometimes their gain is money. In this particular story it seems to have been for control, perhaps for prestige, but certainly for control of the mind and soul of Sergius, the proconsul, who was like a governor of that territory.

There are magicians who traffic in illusion in our day. One is the media, particularly advertisers. Every single one of us, I suspect, watches TV, so powerful because we can both hear and see it. Some of the products that are advertised seem to suggest that physical beauty is definitely desirable. If only we can have it, everything's going to be wonderful. We can marry the person of our dreams and live happily ever after. Life will be beautiful.

Furthermore, if we buy product X sold by a particular advertiser, we can achieve beauty. So some advertisers can be part of the magicland where the name of the game is basically illusion. And of course they represent business people who are out to make a profit. Not all of that is bad, but how much do we allow ourselves to buy into the process?

Another kind of magician I think we see—and this hurts because I have looked at the enemy and she is ME—can be composers. Composers frequently like to please, and such motivation has its positive side. We are not human if, at times, we don't like to do that, but some of us write the kind of music we know will be instantly gratifying to an element of response in almost everybody. I suspect that we do this sometimes not to serve them but to serve ourselves. A flood of instantly gratifying music is available on today's market. I'm sure you know how hard it is to find a good piece of music in a stack of 10. By good, I mean one that will say something of quality in all times and all places, will speak to the whole person, and will contain some sort of mystical element that simply can't be duplicated by just anybody. Composers, too, may at times traffic in illusion.

We should not put the blame so often on our publishers of music or on our retailers. They, too, are business people. They are rightly in business to make a profit as well as to serve the public. And they will sell what we will buy.

There is a third institution that sometimes deals in illusion, and that is the church we love. Here again we have our "Simons," our magicians trafficking in illusion. How many times have we heard about church growth and how important numbers are? We even bring in church growth experts to tell our staffs and congregations how many singers need to be in the choirs in order to have certain multiples of those numbers in the congregation. Many of these consultants mean well but still tell us some things that we are only too ready to hear, siren songs that are on the verge of illusion—tell us, even, what kind of music we should be singing and how many choirs should be singing it. I know some that say we should be singing only upbeat, peppy music—as if there could always be an Easter without a Good Friday!

Carl Schalk, in a recent article in *The Christian Century* wrote some potent words on this subject. Professor Schalk is a composer, a teacher, and a church musician. He wrote the music for the hymns "God of the Sparrow" and "Now" and many anthems with which you are familiar. The issue to which I refer appeared March 21, 1990.

Included in what he said were statements having to do with what he called pragmatism and consumerism, mental states to which church growth experts are appealing. Pragmatism asks about our church activity, "Does it get results?" Are we attracting people? How many? A successful music program would seem to be identified by size and number, not necessarily by quality. We seem to aspire to emulate the fastest-growing and the biggest.

"Consumerism," Dr. Schalk says, "will ask the question, 'How do we compete in the denominational marketplace? Are we giving people what they want?' Such questions reflect basic misunderstandings about worship and music." His conclusion is, "We do not come to worship to shape it to our own ends, but to be shaped by God, who calls us together to hear God's word and share God's meal." So magicians we seem to have with us always, even in the church.

The scriptural story we've talked about so far sounds like bad news. But, as always in the gospel, there is good news. For though this may be your story and my story, primarily this is once again God's story.

Paul rebuked Simon Bar-Jesus, the false prophet, the magician. Then he predicted that Simon would become blind for a while. Interesting, for in a sense he was blind already. God has created life so that untruth and unreality will fail. Those who deal in it ultimately will falter and be blind. The "straight path" that Paul mentions is the straight path that Micah refers to: "What does the Lord require of you but to do justly, to love kindness, and to walk humbly with your God?" The Bible is full of such reminders of God's love and justice.

Remember what God said to Jacob? "I'll never give up on you, Jacob." And Jacob was a scoundrel, a cheat, and a conniver. God finally got to him, though it took a long time. Early on, God blessed him saying, "Through you I will bless your children after you." God, as God had promised, never gave up on that. No wonder Jacob said at Bethel, "Surely the Lord was in this place and I didn't even know it!"

Sergius, the proconsul, was absolutely astonished at Paul's message. He had never heard anything like it. After all, he had been listening to the magician. But he was an intelligent man, and he was searching. The story says that he believed what Paul said.

Certainly illusionists and magicians are present with us even today.

But so is God. Jacob learned it at Bethel. Noah learned it when the floods receded and the rainbow came with God's promise never to destroy his creation again. Moses got wind of it in very concrete form in the tablets at Sinai. God has been present in the prophets and their disturbing words, and supremely, we Christians believe, in the Word made flesh: Jesus—his life, his death, his resurrection, and his Spirit that remains powerfully at work. All we have to do is to trust it. The courage to speak out, as Paul did, as the apostles did finally, will come. Today's Psalm says, "Trust in the Lord and do good. Trust in God, who will act, for the wicked shall be cut off, but those who wait for the Lord shall possess the land." Others are influenced by that witness of trusting obedience.

Who could say it better than Martin Luther in "A Mighty Fortress"?

> *And though this world with devils filled*
> *should threaten to undo us,*
> *We will not fear, for God hath willed*
> *his truth to triumph through us.*

Rise and Shine!

(Preached at Choristers Guild Midwinter Workshop, Dallas, Texas, 1988)

Isaiah 60:1-6

*Arise, shine; for your light has come,
   and the glory of the Lord has risen
      upon you.
For darkness shall cover the earth,
   and thick darkness the people;
but the Lord will arise upon you,
   and his glory will appear over you.
Nations shall come to your light,
   and kings to the brightness of your
      dawn.*

*Lift up your eyes and look around;
   they all gather together, they come
      to you;
your sons shall come from far away,
   and your daughters shall be
      carried on their nurses'
         arms.
Then you shall see and be radiant;
   your heart shall thrill and rejoice,
because the abundance of the sea
      shall be brought to you,
   the wealth of the nations shall
      come to you.
A multitude of camels shall cover
      you,
   the young camels of Midian and
      Ephah;
   all those from Sheba shall come.
They shall bring gold and frankincense
   and shall proclaim the praise of
      the Lord.*

What better time than the day after Epiphany Day and those days following that wonderful celebration for Choristers Guild members and all church musicians, for that matter, to consider with their minds, their hearts, their ears, and eyes what that light, that revelation, that manifestation, that epiphany of God might mean?

The lesson from Isaiah set my memory spinning back to what my parents used to say to me on a winter's morning when I was still in the bed half asleep. "Rise and shine! It's morning!" That was bad news. I knew down deep in my skull somewhere that Mother and Daddy were preparing me for the day that was inevitably out there; and of course, to get going I had first to get up. Like the Good News, such an exhortation is always a combination of judgment and mercy, confrontation and forgiveness. But I didn't want to hear "Rise and shine" right then.

Later on I learned another "Rise and shine," and it came by way of Mr. Handel. When I was taking voice in college, I had to work on the solo, "And the glory of the Lord," and I got a different feeling about rising and shining. I began to understand what it meant. Amazing, isn't it, how music can do that?

This time, when I got ready to do what I'm doing right now with you, I looked at that text again. All of a sudden the pronouns jumped out at me. What would happen if the pronouns were emphasized and we thought about this as if it were: "Arise, shine; for *your* light has come, and the glory of the Lord has risen upon *you*"? "And His glory will be seen upon *you*"? "The wealth of the nations shall come to *you*"?

Who, me? Us—because it really is "us." When the Bible says "you," most of the time, as John Deschner, a colleague of mine at Southern Methodist University, likes to put it, it means "you-all." It's addressing the people of God. So when God chooses to reveal Godself and God's ways, God says, "Arise, shine, you-all; my glory will be seen upon you *all.*" Doesn't God use strange events and strange people sometimes as a means of doing that? Moses, Jacob, those unbelieving disciples who were so much like us and who didn't quite get it until later on? A baby in a manger? This baby is God's epiphany?

But good news it was. Rise and shine—out of those warm bedclothes of safety and dependency—"for *your* light, *YOUR* light has come." "Lift up your eyes and see," it goes on to say. Isn't that what we do? All we have to do is look, to break away somehow from that tunnel vision that just sees the world of routine and headlines, to see with our heads, as another colleague, Dick Murray, likes to put it. When the Bible says "see," it usually means perceive, see with your head.

What can help us do that? One of those aids to seeing, for instance, is information. That's why we're all here today. Study, workshops, recordings, biblical words, good literature, plays, education of all kinds—revelation comes in both sacred and secular forms. In the movie, "The Verdict" with Paul Newman, which to me was an epiphany story, brilliant light flooded the scene every time truth was evident, but much of the story was filmed in very dark settings because the truth Newman was trying to uncover was deeply buried.

Information is one of the aids to seeing. Imagination is another. How can we express the inexpressible without it? No wonder the Bible is written in metaphors that sometimes are difficult to translate. Imagination and information and scholarship are all required. Art forms help convey the inexpressible profoundly—music, dancing, painting, symbols. Think of that butterfly at Easter—what better symbol? The Wise Men themselves represent the revelation of Godself to the whole world, not just to those people we call the chosen people, but to everybody else as well.

What would happen if we had the imagination to look at our choir members as they might become, as well as who they are? Imagination is important. Intellect, insight, and industry are other "I" words that apply, too.

The most important word, however, is not an "I" word. It is trust. Those Wise Men saw with the eyes of faith, the eyes of trust. They didn't know exactly what they were going to find, but they knew they were going to find something at the end of their search. Not everybody saw the star. Not everybody had the imagination *or* the trust. Not everybody saw Jesus after the Resurrection either, but the people who trusted did. Seeing that star, seeing Jesus, meant perceiving with information and imagination, but it also meant trusting that these pointed to some sort of revelation. That revelation turned out to be salvation.

Those shepherds and Wise Men both looked. They trusted. And then they did what we have to do, or what we are invited to do—never forced to do—by God, and that's to make a decision about the Light. For that gift, that Light of the World, was, and is, already there, freely given, and waiting for us to embrace.

The Church, you see, bets its life. It's made a decision: you-all, we-all, the Church. We've bet our lives that that baby and the way he lived and died is, indeed, God's epiphany, a window for seeing what God and living under God's rule and love and power really are like. Our fears then are overcome and we can dare to risk—in our jobs, schools, homes, in all of our work and play. What we can do alone is not the last word about us at all.

"All creation will come to you," the story says, "from far and near." It will come to *you-all*. So we *don't* all have degrees. So we *can't* perform perfectly; but we keep working and looking. We remember that the scripture says, "Lift up your eyes and see." We keep adding information. We keep studying and learning. We keep using our imaginations, for we are dealing in art forms. We do our music in order to help ourselves and others understand with the heart what that good news is about, because we are dealing with beauty. And now and then a light surprises, and we are given that insight that helps us to trust with the eyes of faith.

"The glory of the Lord has risen in *you-all*." So in us the light shines in reflection just as the sun, before it comes over the horizon in the morning, throws its light on the clouds in the west. Have you ever had the experience of seeing those clouds? They're pink. And you know the sun is opposite them, even when it has not quite appeared.

Are we not the pink clouds, if the glory of the Lord has risen in us all? Pink clouds are beautiful and mean so much to everyone. How amazing! We can make our music and do our work knowing that.

To the Mountain and Back

(Preached at American Guild of Organists service, Baton Rouge, Louisiana, 1984)

One of the most fascinating and beautiful, yet puzzling, stories in the gospels of Matthew, Mark, and Luke is the transfiguration story. I read and reread it recently, partly because it captured me and I couldn't leave it alone, and partly because I wanted to see if it had a particular word for church musicians and artists.

Matthew in the seventeenth chapter of his gospel lays out the story dramatically. Jesus takes Peter, James, and John and climbs one of the mountains near Caesarea Philippi, possibly to get away from the crowds and rest, perhaps to do some serious thinking about the implications of his ministry, pointing as they did toward a cross. At the top the disciples suddenly see the vision of Jesus, his face radiant, his body clothed in purest white, talking with Moses and Elijah, the representatives of the law and prophetic tradition. Awestruck, and excited to be witnesses to such a vision, they babble among themselves, searching for a response appropriate to the occasion and finally coming up with Peter's extravagant offer to build three booths, or tabernacles, on the spot to honor Jesus, Moses, and Elijah. (Mark's comment on Peter's over-reaction is, "For he did not know what to say.")

While they are still stammering, a bright cloud comes over them, and the voice of God speaks out of it the same words heard at Jesus' baptism: "This is my beloved Son. Listen to him." By this time the disciples are on the ground, quaking with fear. But Jesus comes over to them, touches them, and says, "Get up. Do not be afraid." As they look up, they see Jesus only, appearing simply as the friend and teacher they had accompanied up the mountain; so they get themselves up and start the trek back down into the valley and thence to work, doubtless unheeding of Jesus' command to say nothing about the experience for the time being.

The compelling part of the story at first glance is the experience of the ecstatic vision. Yet who of us, handling the raw materials of ecstasy as we do almost daily as we go about the business of making music or describing beauty by means of other arts, has not at one time or another heard an anthem sung so beautifully or an organ fugue of Bach played so sublimely or an idea depicted visually so movingly that we have caught a peek of eternity? Or know a rehearsal to go so well that we suddenly realize that the church is indeed of God and our choir capable at least on some occasions of angelic sound? Or had a worship experience that strangely warmed the heart without warning, showing us, if only dimly and momentarily, what the Creator may have had in mind when we were first formed from clay?

Moments of ecstasy are not limited to artists or church-goers. They happen to us all in our personal and communal lives: lovers know magic moments when all is right with their romance and hence the world; parents experience visions of what their children can be during those fleeting seconds when they look and act so dear; citizens can catch a vision of an America as it was meant to be as they witness a patriotic event or visit a national shrine. Our visions are important, for they remind us of what can be, indeed of how God can break through our history and present eternity to us when God is least expected. Visions keep us on track when the going gets rough, and the memory of them sustains us through discouraging times, as doubtless the memory of the transfiguration vision stiffened the spine of the disciples during the dark days of Holy Week and beyond, reminding them that God indeed had put a stamp of approval on Jesus' life and work.

Mountain-top experiences have their flip side, however. The feelings we thrill to at the time are so wonderful we're tempted to hang onto them for dear life, living in memories and attempting to freeze the moments for all time. Peter wanted to put up monuments. We take a picture or make a recording of the inspirational event. Perpetuating these moments on film or tape can be enjoyable and downright helpful if it inspires us realistically. But often it can set us to looking backward at what has happened, so that we lose interest in getting on with the reality of living in the moment or dealing with the future. Nostalgia is also a solo pursuit in which we revel in our own personal feelings. Dreaming wistfully of a past experience, no matter how exhilarating, can isolate us from the needs of others.

As a composer, I much prefer the moments, rare though they are, of inspiration and creativity to the hours of tedious notation, arranging, and proofreading. They are heady moments, those inspirational ones, and composition would be drudgery without them. But until the music I dream up gets into written form where it can be accessible to others who will perform it and hear it, my heady moments of inspiration are centered only in me and keep me and the music trapped, walled off from relationship to anyone else. Artists, organists, and choir directors know well how tempting it is likewise to bask in the memories and tapes of past performances or rehearsals and put off the tough business of getting on with making music and art for times and audiences now and in the future.

God's words out of the cloud would seem to be pointing not backward to the mountaintop vision, but forward to the reality of life and work in the valley. "Listen to him," God says of the beloved Son. And what do we hear if we listen? The very first words Jesus is quoted as saying in the story itself are, "Don't be afraid. Get up." They deal with the present reality of a quite natural fear and then point ahead to the need to be about the work down the mountain. He utters no great words of power or pomp befitting one envisioned conversing with the high dignitaries of heaven, Moses and Elijah, but a reassuring word of healing and a reminder that it is time to roll up sleeves and get back to the business of ministry where there will be suffering to endure. With these words Jesus does what in biblical language means love and restoration: he touches the disciples. His words are vividly reinforced by that action.

It is this final half of the story—the down-to-earth part—that carries such power, it seems to me. Our visions are gifts from God—indeed, maybe God's method of breaking into our history in a dramatic way—and necessary as memories of the sublime moments that can hearten and inspire us. But our calling is down in the valley, doing our job unafraid and ministering to those in our care—family, congregations, fellow-citizens. Jesus' words, which God urges us to listen to, invariably have to do with loving the neighbor, being healed and forgiven, trusting. His stories of the prodigal son, the ninety-and-nine, the talents, the good Samaritan, and others say it over and over again, and his life, death, and resurrection attest to it.

We revel in our feelings, just like Peter and his friends. We even fail time and again to understand the meaning of ecstatic moments, just like the disciples. Yet Jesus, knowing this, continues to hold us all close, calming our fears, urging us to live and work with him, and overlooking our weaknesses. What can be more reassuring than this?

Working as a church artist or musician presents from time to time rare opportunities for experiencing visions of unspeakable beauty that bring God closer and suggest that eternity is truly a possibility. But the work down in the valley of our realities is moving pianos, studying scores, tuning reeds, hanging banners, memorizing lines and movements, sitting in staff meetings, loving the choristers who seem bent on being unlovable, and wrestling with our own doubts and discouragements throughout. A transfiguration story tells us that God sets a seal on us and on our work and is there loving us amid our stumblings, assuring us that the outcome is ultimately in God's hands, not ours—Good News indeed.

Chosen: A Symphony in Three Movements

(Preached at Northaven United Methodist Church, Dallas, Texas, July 1991)

II Samuel 7:1-17

Now when the king was settled in his house, and the Lord had given him rest from all his enemies around him, the king said to the prophet Nathan, "See now, I am living in a house of cedar, but the ark of God stays in a tent." Nathan said to the king, "Go, do all that you have in mind; for the Lord is with you."

But that same night the word of the Lord came to Nathan: Go and tell my servant David: Thus says the Lord: Are you the one to build me a house to live in? I have not lived in a house since the day I brought up the people of Israel from Egypt to this day, but I have been moving about in a tent and a tabernacle. Wherever I have moved about among all the people of Israel, did I ever speak a word with any of the tribal leaders of Israel, whom I commanded to shepherd my people Israel, saying, "Why have you not built me a house of cedar?" Now therefore thus you shall say to my servant David: Thus says the Lord of hosts: I took you from the pasture, from following the sheep to be prince over my people Israel; and I have been with you wherever you went, and have cut off all your enemies from before you; and I will make for you a great name, like the name of the great ones of the earth. And I will appoint a place for my people Israel and will plant them, so that they may live in their own place, and be disturbed no more; and evildoers shall afflict them no more, as formerly, from the time that I appointed judges over my people Israel; and I will give you rest from all your enemies. Moreover the Lord declares to you that the Lord will make you a house. When your days are fulfilled and you lie down with your ancestors, I will raise up your offspring after you, who shall come forth from your body, and I will establish his kingdom. He shall build a house for my name, and I will establish the throne of his kingdom forever. I will be a father to him, and he shall be a son to me. When he commits iniquity, I will punish him with a rod such as mortals use, with blows inflicted by human beings. But I will not take my steadfast love from him, as I took it from Saul, whom I put away from before you. Your house and your kingdom shall be made sure forever before me; your throne shall be established forever. In accordance with all these words and with all this vision, Nathan spoke to David.

Mark 6:1-6

He left that place and came to his hometown, and his disciples followed him. On the sabbath he began to teach in the synagogue, and many who heard him were astounded. They said, "Where did this man get all this? What is this wisdom that has been given to him? What deeds of power are being done by his hands! Is not this the carpenter, the son of Mary and brother of James and Joses and Judas and Simon, and are not his sisters here with us?" And they took offense at him. Then Jesus said to them, "Prophets are not without honor, except in their hometown, and among their own kin, and in their own house." And he could do no deed of power there, except that he laid his hands on a few sick people and cured them. And he was amazed at their unbelief.

II Corinthians 12:1-10

It is necessary to boast; nothing is to be gained by it, but I will go on to visions and revelations of the Lord. I know a person in Christ who fourteen years ago was caught up to the third heaven—whether in the body or out of the body I do not know; God knows. And I know that such a person—whether in the body or out of the body I do not know; God knows—was caught up into Paradise and heard things that are not to be told, that no mortal is permitted to repeat. On behalf of such a one I will boast, but on my own behalf I will not boast, except of my weaknesses. But if I wish to boast, I will not be a fool, for I will be speaking the truth. But I refrain from it, so that no one may think better of me than what is seen in me or heard from me, even considering the exceptional character of the revelations. Therefore, to keep me from being too elated, a thorn was given me in the flesh, a messenger of Satan to torment me, to keep me from being too elated. Three times I appealed to the Lord about this, that it would leave me, but he said to me, "My grace is sufficient for you, for power is made perfect in weakness." So, I will boast all the more gladly of my weaknesses, so that the power of Christ may dwell in me. Therefore I am content with weaknesses, insults, hardships, persecutions, and calamities for the sake of Christ; for whenever I am weak, then I am strong.

To be chosen, hand-picked, singled out of the group for something special is to feel like shouting "Hip-hip-hooray!" to the world. The recognition doesn't have to be newsworthy; it can be a small thing, even unexpected. But it is a wonderful experience for the one chosen, worth a lusty "Hooray!" or in Bible language, "Hosanna!"

I remember well the first time it happened to me. A six-year-old first-grader, I was a wimpy, weepy, anxious little girl who hated school because it meant leaving Mother and safety, and I lived for the bell ending the school day. One bright spot, however, in Mary Delle

Cowser's homeroom was the unit on building furniture out of orange crates. When Miss Cowser pulled out the crates and distributed real tools so we could begin the hammering and sawing, I perked up a little. And the day Miss Cowser said, "Jane Anne will be assigned the saw, for she can saw a straight line so well," was such a red-letter one for me that I recall the feeling of "Hip-hip-hooray, Hosanna!" vividly after 60 years.

I had been hand-picked, singled out from my classmates for that small job, and from then on during those few weeks, I couldn't wait for the orange crates and tools to appear. My self-esteem had skyrocketed, and I now had something to shout about, at least inwardly.

What it means to be chosen by God is the subject addressed in the lessons suggested by the Common Lectionary these summer Sundays, and we hit the "Hosanna" aspect right away in the Old Testament story about David. David, having brought together the tribes of Israel in what begins to shape up as a nation, sits, during a relatively peaceful interval, on the throne in his impressive house of cedar—truly a castle. The Ark of the Covenant, however, remains unhoused, and since the Ark represents the Presence of God, David proposes, "Lord, I will make you a house!"—a house befitting the Deity.

God's answer, in paraphrase, is: "David, remember I chose you, a simple shepherd boy, and brought you to the place of honor you hold today." And then the wonderful play on words: "Besides, says God, I haven't had a house during all these years since I brought your people out of bondage in Egypt; and I've managed. It is I, David, who will make you a house"—meaning the head of a dynasty, a line, a family, a Community—"a house that will live into eternity. Your offspring can make me a house"—this is a temple—which, as we know, Solomon did. Grounds for a grand "Hosanna!" from David, and certainly one from us Christians looking back 2,000 years to that descendant of David, that descendant who rode into Jerusalem on a donkey to the people's shouts of "Hosanna to the Son of David!" David, the chosen; Jesus the supreme Chosen One for Christians—Jesus, who has made all of us now God's chosen; "honorary Jews," as Virgil Howard, one of my colleagues at Perkins School of Theology, puts it.

This is a hosanna to be shouted, sung, danced, played, painted, and prayed, the natural and right human responses to an honor virtually unbelievable to us 20th-century rationalist Americans, who have been taught that we should get only what we earn. And it is the initial movement in this three-movement symphony of salvation.

But now comes a short intermission while the mutes can be put on the strings and into the horns. "Hosanna" is not all there is, as we quickly find out in the models the New Testament lessons lay out for us.

"A prophet," Jesus says in Mark's gospel, "is recognized and honored everywhere but at home, among his own folks." This supreme Chosen One is rejected, thought to be crazy by some of his own family, and faced with the realization that his teaching is not accepted by those he knows best. One can hear the townspeople of Nazareth saying derisively, "This is Joe's kid? The carpenter's son? Come on!" One can assume many said the same kind of thing about Lincoln: "Nancy Hanks' boy? That long-legged kid who split logs and told funny stories—President? Are you kidding?" So chosenness means hurt as well as hosanna, and it is this hurt that is the second movement of the symphony, the one that provides the contrast in the grand scheme of things. King David himself knew the hurt that was added to his earlier hosanna as he grieved over the betrayal and then the death of his son Absalom.

Is there any parent that does not know both these feelings, hosanna and hurt, that are woven into the fabric of parenthood? Friends and lovers know them, too, as do those hand-picked for special responsibility in our various communities. "Why the hurt?" we ask, echoing that singular prophet of our time, Lucy, in the gospel recounted in "Peanuts." "Why do I have to have ups and down?" she screams. "Why can't my life be ups, ups, and more ups?" (Robert L. Short, *The Gospel According to Peanuts*; John Knox Press, 1965.)

During the next brief intermission, while the strings and horns remove their mutes, St. Paul strides onto the stage, and we begin to get an answer to that question with the downbeat of the last movement of the symphony.

Hurt can be an antidote to arrogance, Paul tells us, remembering the ecstatic visions he was chosen to have and had grounds to boast about, at least from the world's point of view. "But God sent me a thorn in the flesh," he says, "and when three times I asked God to remove it, the answer was, "Paul, my grace is sufficient for you." Were it not for the pain of the thorns, Paul goes on to explain, he would have become so arrogant and self-important he'd have focused only on his own ego and not on those to whom he was called to minister, probably not even on God. So his boasting, then, was justified only by his weakness, his hurt; for because of it he had to cast himself in faith on God alone—the God who promised him grace sufficient for anything life could throw at him, be it thorns, persecution, rejection, even death: cause for the loudest "Hosanna!" of all, since, as he says elsewhere, nothing could separate him—nor can it separate us—from the love of God in Christ Jesus.

Hand-picked by God means hand-held by God, and with all the cherubim and seraphim we can pull out the stops and join in that third movement, the return of "Hosanna!"—this time *fortissimo*. The symphony is composed by God, and we are hand-picked by God, as David was hand-picked out of the fields to be the founder of a house that would lead into eternity, as Jesus was hand-picked to be the vessel by which our salvation would be most lovingly freighted—Jesus, whose week of triumphal entry into Jerusalem, crucifixion, then resurrection was the model-in-the-flesh for this symphony with its three movements of

Hosanna, Hurt, Hosanna.

A most beautiful illustration of this reality is Chaim Potok's novel *The Chosen* (Simon and Schuster, 1967) made soon after its publication into a movie. Old Reb Saunders, the tzaddik, or leader, of the small community of Hasidic Jews living in New York City during the mid-20th century, has a brilliant son Daniel, expected, like his father before him, to become a rabbi and tzaddik of his people. But Reb Saunders raises his son in silence, never speaking to him except in Talmud class, a state of affairs the boy accepts because he honors and reveres his father but nevertheless endures with much suffering. When Daniel makes friends with another bright Jewish boy, Reuven, who is not a member of the Hasidic community and much more liberal, the old rabbi refuses to allow the friendship to continue, thus hurting both boys. Near the close of the story the three come together in Reb Saunders' study, and the rabbi explains.

When Daniel was four years old, he says, Daniel read a story about suffering people, and the boy, having a photographic memory, repeated the story word for word proudly to his father, but without showing a shred of compassion for the people in the book.

> I went away and cried to the Master of the Universe, "What have you done to me? A mind like this I need for a son? A heart I need for a son, a soul I need for a son, compassion I want for my son, righteousness, mercy, strength to suffer and carry pain, that I want from my son, not a mind without a soul!"

So he goes on to explain his reason, right or wrong, for the silence and for separating the two friends.

> "One learns of the pain of others by suffering one's own pain...by turning inside oneself, by finding one's own soul. And it is important to know of pain. It destroys our self-pride, our arrogance, our indifference toward others....Better I should have had no son at all than to have a brilliant son who had no soul....I have no more fear now....My Daniel has learned."

And then both the loving old father and the brilliant son embrace and weep for joy. "Hosanna!" returns.

Chosen: Hosanna, Hurt, Hosanna—a symphony of salvation in three movements. The Alpha and the Omega, the first and last Word, and all in between, are God's. For to be God's hand-picked is to be God's hand-held. This is God's doing, and it is marvelous in our eyes.

A Lost 'Te Deum'

(Keynote address delivered at the Convocation of the Hymn Society of America, Dallas, Texas, 1979)

Last fall the committee put together to plan this opening service of the Hymn Society's convocation began to meet. At one of those first meetings it was decided to use the great hymn of the church, the "Te Deum Laudamus," the "praise to God," as a liturgical framework for the service. The chairman gave each of us a copy of the translation of the Te Deum text with annotations in the margin to help suggest what service music, hymns, and anthems appropriate to each of the lessons we might consider using. The annotated Te Deum was our working paper, the stuff of which this service is made. It was important. It was valuable. And we would use it through the winter and into the spring as we prepared for this occasion.

After that first meeting I took my copy of the Te Deum and put it in the car along with other lists—grocery lists and lists of errands that I had to do—and took off to do those errands before going home to get dinner ready. I stopped at a mailbox and got out to mail some letters. It was a very windy, gusty day and a lot of letters that I had on the seat of the car blew out the door as I got out. I retrieved them, I thought, and went on about my business, finished my errands, and went home.

It was later that evening that I discovered my Te Deum was missing. I went into panic. I looked through everything, under the seats of the car, in the garage. I retraced my steps to see if that valuable piece of paper was anywhere that I had stopped. No luck, I didn't find it.

Now that was just one instance of a lost Te Deum. How many thousands of times per day it must happen, at least metaphorically. Change a few minor details and I expect you could have been reading out of my diary. It is not hard in days like this to lose the impulse to praise, to breathe alleluias of gratitude and thanksgiving, to shout "Holy, holy, holy" to the God of power and might with the bounce and buoyancy worthy of human beings, let alone cherubim and seraphim.

Do you remember losing your Te Deum? Well, let me put it to you this way: do you work in a church?

Have you ever found it hard to accentuate the positive and mean it as you dealt with your youth, for instance? I have a friend who has loved and taught young people in church school for 25 years. She says that they have never been as hard to reach as they are now. When she asks them to write down on a piece of paper what their dominant feeling is, they write "tired." When she asks who their heroes are, they say "not any." The two words that seem to turn them off, she says, are "God" and "Bible." So she must find a biblical, unbiblical way to get the Gospel through to them. Does this describe your youth choir or some of the young people in it?

A director friend told me not too long ago that he was sure that if it weren't for handbells he would have no youth active in music in his church. Did you ever hang your guitar on a willow tree and weep when you remembered how it used to be with youth choirs in Zion and your church? It's easy to lose a Te Deum, isn't it, in light of the situation with today's young people?

Perhaps you have served on an organ committee. Have you ever found it hard to celebrate life as a church musician and praise the Lord in the middle of a meeting in which three-fourths of your committee and perhaps the chairman of the new building committee and the architect as well are convinced that a church is not a church without carpet and that organ pipes should be heard and not seen? A Te Deum can get lost pretty easily in that kind of shuffle.

Some of you may have moved into a congregation that knows almost none of the hymns that you know or even wants to learn them. Can you join the glorious company of the apostles in singing "Te Deum Laudamus" then? I know a director who moved from New England to a small town in Texas to serve a church of the same denomination. During the first service in Advent she watched the hymn book covers close, one by one, on every single hymn she had picked, including "Come, Thou Long-Expected Jesus" and "O Come, O Come, Emmanuel," which, they told her later, they really did not know. In times like these a Te Deum can get misplaced.

Or you may have felt, if you are a pastor or teacher or musician in the church, that you worked so intensely and long in planning and executing the liturgy that you were almost vaccinated against its moving you personally to any kind of thanksgiving and exultation except to experience the satisfaction of a job reasonably well done. Don't we wish for a shout of sacred joy to well up in *us* at 11 o'clock some Sunday mornings?

To work in a church certainly is to know what it means to lose a Te Deum. But then, to be alive in this world does, too. We all know well the dismal stories that appear in the newspaper and on TV every day that reach beyond the troubles of our own vocation. Terrorism, the cost of living, war, racial discrimination, gender discrimination, air-ear-soul pollution, original sin: a long list of hobgoblins and foul fiends stifles our praise, smothers gratitude, and sends our Te Deums into hiding; the list is depressingly familiar.

What do you do when you lose your Te Deum? The friends and disciples of Jesus we read about in our lessons for this Easter season must have asked the same question many times after the crucifixion. What is so striking in the Gospel accounts is their response to these events: it is so very much like our own; that is, it is so human. What did they do? In those days immediately following the murder of Jesus they remembered and they wept. Mary wept in the garden that first day of the week, remembering the one that had changed her life. The little gaggle of friends hid that evening for fear of the Jews, remembering what their friend Jesus had talked about and done. One can imagine how the memories of good times and bad times together came flooding back, along with some of Jesus' stories and words and actions, many of which probably suddenly came clear for the first time; because those disciples just didn't get the whole picture, as many times as Jesus tried to portray it while he was alive.

Memories like theirs are not unlike some of ours. I am reminded of the evening of November 22, 1963, the date President Kennedy was shot in Dallas. Those of us who supported and admired Kennedy had planned a party at our house that night. I had nothing to do with the Kennedy visit to Dallas that day; it was coincidental that we had planned the party for that night. We decided, in the midst of our grief and shock, that we would go ahead and have our dinner because it would help us to get together as friends who shared the same political feelings. We could comfort each other. One's community helps at a time like that, when Te Deums get buried.

And yet, as we read of those disciples, we learn that in the midst of those very human responses of tears and fears, the Presence suddenly was there among them, as he had appeared to Mary at the tomb and to Thomas later when he said, "Here, feel for yourself!" (It's human, of course, to doubt as well as it is to fear and grieve.) So, while they wept and feared and doubted and remembered as the truly human beings they were, the Presence was among them in some inexpressible way. And they were restored and renewed.

The disciples and friends of Jesus also went on about the business of living. They did their jobs. Their leader and reason for rejoicing was gone, but there were still hungry mouths to feed, taxes to be collected, fish to be caught, commerce to be dealt with, business trips to take to Emmaus and elsewhere. What's more human than that—to go on, somehow, about the business of living and working whether we feel like it or not? You will remember that in the midst of the fishermen's fishing, to use one example, the Presence came again. Jesus told them to harvest those fish and invited them to join him for breakfast right there on the beach. In the midst of the loss, when a Te Deum must have been almost impossible to muster, the Presence, unexpected and unbidden, was there, even as they mourned and worked—which is to say, even as they dipped deep into their humanity and acted like the real people they were.

Now here we are 20th-century Easter people in the season following that great celebration, with the same human emotions day in and day out—joys and experiences of great happiness, bewilderment, loss, doubt, anger—just like those early Christians. I can think of no group of present-day Christians, who, in their remembering and their work and their worship, are surrounded by so great a cloud of witnesses as are members of a Hymn Society. We handle, week in and week out, the materials of the faith, don't we—the texts of our brothers and sisters as well as their notes and rhythms? These are the brothers and sisters that testify again and again to that love, that Presence, among them then and among us now, that makes us able to lift an alleluia, to find our Te Deums—a love that, even though it did not remove the problems or erase the losses, shared them, and in sharing them made possible a strength necessary to handle those agonies to which all flesh, being grass, is heir. A witness like that 15th-century poet who said:

> *O love, how deep, how broad, how high,*
> *How passing thought and fantasy*
> *That God, the Son of God, should take*
> *Our mortal form for mortals' sake.*

Or our brother William Blake, who said:

> *He becomes a man of woe;*
> *He doth feel the sorrow, too.*
> *Till our grief is fled and gone,*
> *He doth sit by us and moan.*

Or that black psalmist who wrote:

> *Jesus walked this lonesome valley;*
> *He had to walk it by himself.*

Or that fearless Christian witness Dietrich Bonhoffer, executed by the Nazis for collaborating to kill Hitler:

> *We go to God when God is sore bestead:*
> *Find God poor and scorned, without shelter or bread;*
> *Whelmed under weight of the wicked, the weak, and the dead.*

or Claudia Hernamann:

> *As thou did'st hunger bear, and thirst*

so teach us, gracious Lord,
To die and to self and chiefly live
by thy most holy word.

What do you remember when you lose your Te Deum?

Are you with me when I say that I remember, with a lot of help from my friends from this community, a Lord who knew what it was *not* to feel like singing? Who cried for his friends, for his city, and for himself? Who asked that the cup pass? On my manuscript of the old mass words hanging on my wall, done by the monks back in some century long ago, everything is in black except one statement: *"Et homo factus est:"* "and became man." It is in bright red. No wonder! We go on singing, whether we feel like it or not. We go on working with the same youth choirs, the same committees, in the same buildings, on the same organs, with the same hymn books, and for the good of the same world.

And like that experience in that upstairs room or among the fisherfolk on the beach, sometimes a light does surprise Christians while they sing. The last word about us is not our grief, our lost Te Deums, our anger, our befuddlement, or anything else in all creation. We can say our Te Deum is found. Te Deum Laudamus!

Lessons of Grace

Plastic Spoons or Sterling?

(Printed in MCC Communique, the newsletter of the Mesquite Civic Chorus, Summer 1990. Used by permission.)

In a gathering of choir directors recently, after we'd discussed the need to choose music of high quality for our groups, a young man stood and asked hesitantly, "Jane, exactly what *is* good music?" Many of us think we are pretty clear about knowing what good music is when we hear it, but articulating the definition in a sentence or two without much warning is another matter. I punted. "Come back tomorrow," I said, "and we'll talk about it."

That night in my motel room I was trying to frame an intelligent answer when my eye fell on the plastic spoon I keep in my make-up kit just in case I'm lucky enough as I travel to discover a supermarket nearby that can supply a pint of my oldest and dearest vice, ice cream. The spoon began to speak to me, so I decided to take it with me to rehearsal the next morning so the choir folks could be privy to the results of our conversation.

Why, for example, was that plastic spoon any different from any of the sterling spoons I had at home—the ones my mother had handed down to me? It was the same shape. It handled my ice cream very nicely. It wasn't heavy. It was a very handy item.

But would I want to hand it down to my children?

That next morning we all agreed, of course, that the answer to that was "No," and I left the group with no more answer than that—simply the memory of that plastic spoon, hoping it would tickle their questioning intellects and mine further and stimulate some valuable responses as the years passed.

Why would I not want to hand that spoon down to my children? That's the next question, of course, and to answer that, without pressing the analogy too far, is to begin to answer the original, "What is good music?"

I think there are at least four characteristics of quality—in our case, of good music or any other art.

An obvious one is *universality*. Good music speaks to people everywhere. A simple Chinese folk melody is just as hauntingly beautiful to Australian or American ears as it is to Chinese. The music of tribal dances from Kenya will set toes tapping in New Jersey and New Guinea.

The Tokyo Philharmonic plays Mozart as lovingly as the New York Philharmonic does, and audiences respond with equal affection. The sounds good music makes are a common language. My sterling spoons will work under any conditions anywhere. My plastic one is so fragile it will break on anything but the softest food, and it will melt in the dishwasher.

Good music or art is also *timeless*. It connects not only people in all places but people in all ages as well. The same elements of pitch and rhythm and structure that we hear in today's music were present in the chants and incantations of the ancient world, as they were in the tones of the Renaissance. A French cathedral choir can sing Poulenc and Gregorian chant in what amounts to the same breath, certainly in one sitting, and the congregation worships, sensing its kinship with the communion of saints past and present. In some of our American hymnals the tunes of Bach, Ives, and Duke Ellington appear along with wonderful old American shape-note melodies like WARRENTON for "Come, Thou Fount." Art is no more limited by time than it is by place. My sterling has been used by past generations and will be used by Marshalls to come, and it will only increase in value.

Good music also will *speak to the whole person*. Body, mind, and spirit will become engaged by that art work, not just the intellect, and not just the feelings. We singers all know about "falling in love" instantly with a piece that appeals immediately to the senses. The piece may have a catchy melody or captivating rhythm easily grasped. But for some reason we tire of it quickly, for there is little there to challenge the mind or imagination. Or we try a work whose appeal is almost totally intellectual, with a few sounds, if any, we can relate to even as we become more familiar with it, and we find it hard to make friends with because our feelings have somehow not been addressed. This is not to say either work should not be done or will not be appropriate at one time or place. But the chances of its becoming a part of us or of others down the years are slim, precisely because it has appealed to only one aspect of our being. My silver spoons are not only functional, they are beautiful to look at and feel; they satisfy both my physical and my emotional, or esthetic, needs.

Finally, good music will *speak uniquely*, that is, in an almost undefinable way that cannot be duplicated. We may call this inspiration or genius or simply mystery. Certainly it is a quality that Robert Shaw has in mind when he talks about those special little black spots on five lines that, translated into sound, exemplify flesh-become-word, or spirit. Salieri, a perfectly competent composer, was not Mozart, any more than the highly skilled sons of Bach were Johann Sebastian. Mozart and Bach both ended periods of musical history, Classical and Baroque, because their music said it all: there was just nothing further anyone could add in those styles. Those who tried ended up as no more than imitators of Bach and Mozart. The works of those giants, like the paintings and sculptures of Michelangelo, the poetry of Frost, or the dramatic cadences of Shakespeare, not to mention spirituals like "Were You There?" or folk songs like "Shenandoah," can exist on their own, almost becoming, as Shaw suggests, objects of our worship themselves. My sterling spoons are different in their pattern and design from any other spoons, and only an artisan silversmith could have produced them. I delight in simply having them.

How do we learn what is finest? By exposure, certainly, like friends-to-be getting to know one another by being together over a long period of time. For musicians this means participating in the music, either by performing it or by listening to it, live or on recordings—the more, and the more widely varied, the better. The beautiful thing about a fine chorus that sings fine music is that it enriches not only the singers but all those who listen as well. The chorus therefore performs a profound service to everyone, for in this day of high-tech hustle and bustle, of geographical and spiritual landscapes polluted with clutter, who would argue that the nourishment that beauty gives is not more essential than ever? And if we who are involved intimately with it don't provide it, who will?

The Passionate Church Musician

(From Church Music Workshop—Practical Tools for Effective Music Ministry, Jan.-Apr. 1991. Copyright © 1991 Abingdon Press. Reprinted by permission.)

"The man has *passion*," my friend said, as together we watched an admired colleague conduct a choral rehearsal. "I tell you, Jane," she went on, shaking her head and frowning, "if we don't have that quality in our music-making, we're dead."

Dead is a strong word, and it has forced me to realize over and over since that day how right she was. Unfortunately, we've limited the use of the word *passion* itself—and therefore our thoughts about it—to romantic behavior, trivialized it by using it to sell exotic perfume on TV, or discarded it as old fashioned. What passion means is caring intensely for something or somebody and showing it in some way. What is it, for instance, that makes one concert or lecture or piece of art more moving, more *right* somehow, than another, given equal conditions of talent and good preparation? It is passion, a deep caring in the artist that vibrates from originator through transmitters to the receivers, or, in musical terms, from composer through performers to listeners.

Passion kindles other human endeavors, too. One thinks immediately of teachers whom we remember best, sprinkled gracefully throughout the classrooms of our childhood and youth. These were invariably the passionate ones, the ones who cared so much about their young subjects and the subject matter they fed us they saw to it that we learned, no matter what techniques it took.

Relationships, too, become solid and lasting when human beings care deeply about each other and somehow manage to reveal that feeling in what they do or say, or both. Administrators and scientists who are effective in their jobs are passionate about their work; they may appear cool and efficient, but they have an inner drive that attacks problems with creativity as fiery as that which influences artists and poets and dancers.

Not surprisingly, passion is a thread running all through the Scriptures, from Old Testament narratives through the Psalms and prophets and into Gospels and Epistles. And certainly Revelation's, "Because you are lukewarm and neither hot nor old, I will spew you out of my mouth," leaves little doubt about the Almighty's opinion.

As church musicians, do we minimize passion's importance? I have done so, especially in my younger days, when I thought I was supposed to be cool. Then I wondered why my music-making as a teacher and conductor wasn't working. I forgot, or didn't know, that talent, scholarship, and techniques without passion were just as bad as passion without talent and preparation. Some of this misunderstanding, or lack of conviction, was simply youthful inexperience and insecurity. However, I think that some of us who teach in college music programs—in our zeal to maintain academe's image of scholarly objectivity—have left, however inadvertently, the impression that information and discipline are worthier than warmth. This is an untruth that is dangerous, and in the arts, at least, downright *deadly*.

Every church musician, having chosen a vocation that is multifaceted, to say the least, must be passionate about at least four different things.

The first is *oneself*, the object of serious caring that often ends up at the bottom of the priority list, if it indeed appears anywhere. Directors of music in local churches have been taught rightly to be passionate about the people they minister to, but all too often they do so at the expense of their own nourishment and health—a state of affairs that in the long run helps nobody. They may fail regularly to take a day off during the week, slight their vacations, forget how to play (recreation), discontinue study, refuse to delegate responsibility to others who can help them in their programs, or get mired so deeply into their jobs they neglect family and friends. Overlooking what a pressure cooker their vocation is, they become targets for burn-out, depression, and all manner of physical ailments, not to mention boredom and cynicism. Being passionate about oneself in a healthy way is not being selfish but the very opposite, as the command to love one's neighbor as one loves oneself assumes. With enlightened self-interest one sees oneself as a part of a good creation that one is responsible for and can enjoy as well.

Part of what this means, for example, is to learn to play and to broaden one's interests. Play, for me, has usually meant work, for I love what I do and would rather be doing church music than anything else I know. (A friend calls this "plerk.") But it is dangerous to make one's play also one's work. Should something happen down the road that makes work impossible, nothing has been cultivated to replace it, and the hole it leaves can eat away at one's well-being. We all ought to have something completely different from our church jobs, I think, that we enjoy doing, whether it's gin rummy, cooking, sports, crosswords, or just plain loafing.

Mental and spiritual stimulation and enrichment in our own area of music and in other disciplines are a must as well. An editor I know has a quote from Goethe on her office wall:

> *One ought at least to hear a little*
> *melody every day,*

*read a fine poem,
see a good picture and,
if possible, make a few sensible remarks.*

Curiosity about, and participation in, the good things of life are so enriching they end up by some amazing grace and chemistry of creation making one's musical being better and the folks a church musician ministers to richer. Contrary to the belief and practice of some, music leaders should not feel guilty for taking time for themselves to rest, play, study, and enjoy, but should feel guilty when they don't.

The second area choir directors must be passionate about is *other people*—staff members with whom they work, singers, instrumentalists, church members, family, and friends inside and outside the church's walls. Some are more naturally pastoral than others, but everyone who undertakes ministry has to take the nurturing of relationships with utter seriousness and work at it constantly, as we all know. This form of passion is *compassion*—thoughtfulness, kindness, understanding, and interest in others. It is manifest in many concrete ways: the music a director selects, knowing how far to push the choir as they sing a varied repertoire, careful pacing of rehearsals, concern about the personal lives of choir members, willingness to bend (surely a requisite for staff meetings!), being sensitive to the congregation's feelings, and honesty in admitting mistakes, to name but a few.

In addition to compassion for others, directors have a third, equally crucial concern: *the art of music itself*. One simply has to be moved and stirred by it, so much so that one is on fire to communicate that excitement to others, both performers and listeners. This does not mean one does not need a breather occasionally, but it does mean that one wants to be deeply involved in it over the long haul. Recently I heard the familiar story of a choir director who tried another profession, one with higher pay, but finally returned to church music because, as he put it, "I missed it too much." When beauty is so vital to the health of us human animals in this day of impersonal technology on an overcrowded planet, the continuing tragedy is that the pay scale in the arts is so low, forcing many either to find another profession or to run themselves ragged moonlighting.

Being passionate about one's music means steady engagement with it; making it; listening to it often, live and on recordings; reading about it and the people who make it; studying the techniques necessary to its effective communication, and imagining in one's mental ear how the particular music one wants to deal with should sound at its best. (This demands solitude that often must be fought for.) For conductors it means perpetual "ear-cleaning" to evaluate accuracy, blend, balance, timbre, and intonation. It means learning about style, history, and performance practice, and certainly developing some appreciation of the other arts. It means cultivating a love for literature, particularly poetry. Selecting and sensitively performing a choral work, even a hymn, without an understanding of the form and content of its text is impossible. It means rigorous attention to conducting techniques, the training of voices separately and in ensemble, and the perfection of diction. It means developing a solid rehearsal pattern that will keep performers busy and alert and will make the whole effort satisfying. All this can help communicate not only the methods of producing the music but also the intense love of the art to others. One of the Almighty's most gracious gifts is music, which enriches the souls of both listeners and performers.

Last, a director needs to be passionate about *the Church*, both the local congregation and the larger Church active throughout the world and the ages. This is true even for those of us who sometimes have a lover's quarrel with the institution's practices or policies—probably that's most of us. Somehow there must be the conviction that in spite of all its fallibility the Church remains an incredibly powerful vehicle for realizing justice, love, and peace on this planet.

One would surely hope all directors know and love the liturgy and are familiar with its expression in history. Liturgy is an art form all by itself, a drama acted out regularly that helps people remember who and whose they are. For musicians who are sensitive in this area, the absence of well-thought-out and well-executed liturgy that springs from solid scriptural, historical, theological, and experiential roots amounts to a little death every Sunday. This most frequently happens when there has not been a team approach among those responsible for planning the service. I know one United Methodist director serving a church whose pastor prefers not to use traditional Wesleyan ritual. Her soul is so starved for beautiful liturgy that she becomes intentionally involved early every Sunday morning with another local church offering a more formal service so she can be liturgically fed. When that kind of passion is channeled into one's own church, everyone is nourished.

Passion for the Church means caring about its mission to the congregation and to all people and helping choirs realize that larger purpose. And it means caring about the Bible and the theology growing from it. The increased use of the lectionary demands this, as does the search for relevant choral music. In children's choirs, where Christian education is part of musical training, little headway can be made if leadership is not knowledgeable. The anthems choirs sing more often than not etch the words of the Bible into singers' minds more deeply than other learning activities do, and truths learned in choir literally become truths to live by for a lifetime.

Finally, it is crucial that directors balance their passion for music, themselves, others, and the Church. To care only about any one area is to lay oneself open to the demons of bitterness and boredom, not to mention fatigue and ill health. The frustration, for instance, of working to make beautiful music with folks who have little professional training can sometimes be almost unbearable unless one has a healthy concern for oneself and a passionate love for the community of the Church as complementary interests.

Much is said, and rightly so, about necessary faith in God—a given we all accept. What can be added is that music itself, when it is the real thing and not a cheap imitation, is worth having faith in, too. It is no exaggeration to say that music, a large mystery within the larger mystery of the Deity itself, is always there to heal and inspire when everything else on earth falls short. That reality is something to be passionate about, a grace note to bless every church musician who has ears to hear.

Priests, Levites, and the Holy

(Perkins Journal, Summer 1985)

I speak as Levite to priests, that is, as a singer of the word to preachers of the word, about a common concern that we have: namely, that act of public worship, central to the life of our congregations, that occurs most frequently on Sunday morning. Now this is a nuts-and-bolts conversation; you won't find it deeply philosophical, but I hope that the nuts and bolts have good solid theological grounding as well as artistic integrity.

Nehemiah's account of worship is a good place to begin. You'll remember that Nehemiah, a member of Artexerxes' administration in Jerusalem, took upon himself the task of getting the wall of Jerusalem rebuilt after the return of the exiles, or more correctly, after the return of the descendants of the exiles, into the city. This is part of that account:

And when the seventh month had come, the children of Israel were in their towns, and all the people gathered as one into the square before the water gate. And they told Ezra the scribe to bring the book of the Law of Moses which the Lord had given to Israel, and Ezra the priest brought the law before the assembly, both men and women and all who could hear with understanding, on the first day of the seventh month. And he read from it, facing the square, before the water gate, from early morning until midday. And the ears of the people were attentive to the Book of the Law. And Ezra the scribe stood on a wooden pulpit which they had made for the purpose, and beside him stood Mattithiah, Shema, Anaiah, Uriah, Hilkiah, and Maaseiah on his right hand, and Pedaiah, Mishael, Malchijah, Hashum, Habaddanah, Zechariah, and Meshullam on his left hand. And Ezra opened the book in the sight of all the people, for he was above the people. And when he opened it all the people stood, and Ezra blessed the Lord the great God, and all the people answered, "Amen, Amen," lifting up their hands; and they bowed their heads and worshiped the Lord with their faces to the ground. The Levites helped the people to understand the Law while the people remained in their places, and they read from the book, from the Law of God, clearly, and they gave the sense, so that the people understood the reading. And Ezra and Nehemiah said, "This day is holy to the Lord your God; do not mourn or weep. Eat the fat and drink sweet wine and send portions to those for whom nothing is prepared, for this day there was a solemn assembly, according to the ordinance. They were assembled with fasting and in sackcloth and with earth upon their heads, and they stood and confessed their sins and the iniquities of their fathers. And then Ezra spoke to the people telling them the wonderful story of their deliverance from captivity and of God's faithfulness to his people, and he implored them to renew their covenant with the Lord their God: and all the people entered into an oath to walk in God's law, and to take upon themselves the obligation to charge themselves yearly with the third part of a shekel for the servants of the house of their God and to bring the first fruits of the ground and of every tree to the house of the Lord.

At the dedication of the wall they sought the Levites to bring them to Jerusalem, to celebrate the dedication with thanksgiving and gladness and with singing and cymbals and harps and lyres. And I commanded the Levites that they should purify themselves and come and guard the gates to keep the Sabbath day holy.

Now I had forgotten, if indeed I ever really knew, that Nehemiah made such good reading on the subject of the public worship of God—so good, in fact, that I found myself leafing through the book with a kind of excitement and anticipation that I normally reserve for Agatha Christie.

One is struck immediately by descriptions of the movements and the moods and personnel in Nehemiah's ceremonies, very similar to those that we know in our own: the moods of adoration, thanksgiving, public confession, the reading of the *Torah*, a sermon and call to action and decision, the response of the offerings, and the taking of the feast to the poor. All these acts were carried out by priests, Levites (those who helped keep the temple and who helped with the worship), and the congregation. Surely we are on the right track, at least, if we are modeling our worship patterns after not only the faithful at Pentecost and Isaiah in the year that King Uzziah died, but now also of Nehemiah.

One is struck, however, by the contrast, all too apparent, between Nehemiah's ceremony and our own Sunday morning ritual. We come off, do we not, rather a poor second? It's clear, it seems to me, that Nehemiah's service is not only a model of the right content and meaning, but a model as well of downright awesome and delightful theater, minutely planned and carefully executed. One can just imagine all the worship commission meetings, all of those conferences with the maintenance folks and the carpenters (they had to get the wooden platform built, for one thing), rehearsals of the singers and instrumentalists and maybe even of dancers, not to mention some pretty persuasive sessions with the keepers of the ecclesiastical purse, that is, the finance commission, for adequate *funding* for this thing.

Why? *Why all this bother?* Certainly, Nehemiah had practical goals in mind. The restoration of morale was pretty high on his list, for the descendants of those exiles had not experienced the oppression in captivity, and therefore had little appreciation for the restoration of the holy places and the holy symbols; not only that: *money* was needed for the maintenance of the holy places. (I can hear you saying, so what else is new?) But were there not deeper reasons? We can assume from reading other accounts in the Old Testament about temple worship that certainly there were: primarily, that for the sensitive Jew, when one worships the Lord God in Israel, one gives it all one's got. Nothing less than one's best—the first fruits—will do. Nothing is left to chance or unrehearsed, to convey the idea and mood of the holy, that is, of the presence of Yahweh in the midst of the people. And to call forth the people's response to that presence, beautiful ceremonial, lovingly prepared and meticulously executed, is required.

"The idea of the holy" calls to mind immediately that old book of Rudolph Otto's of the same title. Many of you read it in seminary, and I notice that those writing about liturgics even today still cite it as a classic reference. You will remember that Professor Otto defines religion as being made up of three essential elements—the devotion to truth, or reality; a commitment to the ethic of love; and an awareness of the *mysterium tremendum*—the great mystery.

How do our worship services reflect these realities—truth, love, and mystery?

We can acknowledge, I think, that we make a pretty good grade in planning and performing those functions in worship that reflect truth and love, especially when doing it verbally; but must not we also acknowledge that our grade point average drops rather severely when it comes to suggesting mystery, the sense of the holy, the "holy other," as a force in our worship?

Whatever happened to mystery?

What indeed has happened to mystery in our daily lives?—not the mystery that we casually refer to ("It's a mystery to me") when we really mean absence of data or information about a subject—that lack that I feel, for instance, in the presence of computer talk, or scientific and technological talk, high or low, or talk of medical science and space. What I mean here is mystery as an awareness, no matter how vague and difficult it may be to describe, of the numinous, of the unfathomable, the ineffably sublime—specifically, of the God who is not only the Father of our Lord Jesus Christ but the Father Almighty, Creator of the universe, who "plants his footsteps in the sea and rides upon the storm" and "whose ways are past finding out." Does *this* God's train still fill our temples? Would we know it if it did? Is it not with *this* God of unbounded love and unimaginable wisdom and power and majesty that all things are possible, even our salvation?

Many of you will also remember an article that appeared in *The*

Christian Century ("Notes on Sacred Space," March 31, 1982) not too many years ago in which the noted church architect E. A. Sövik suggested how our sacred spaces, namely, our church buildings and our sanctuaries, could best express Otto's three elements of religion: truth, love, and mystery. Truth, he says, at least for the church architect, is conveyed by honesty. Love is conveyed by hospitality. And mystery is conveyed by beauty.

Enter here, then, the fine arts. For if architecture can express truth by authenticity, love by hospitality, and mystery by beauty in its concern with space and form, cannot the other arts—drama, dance, music, sculpture, painting, and all the other visual and textile forms—do the same thing in their concern with their media, especially since their approach is through the beautiful? In fact, do we not impoverish ourselves, as we are impoverishing our children in the public schools by phasing out the fine arts? One could wish that we could spend just as much energy in hanging on to the fine arts as we do in wanting to hang on to prayer in the public schools. Do we not impoverish ourselves and our congregations if we do not provide ways for the arts to speak to our senses as well as to our minds—the arts with all their non-verbal eloquence? Is there not power in their ability to touch the emotions, to reach deep within us, even those of us who are untrained—perhaps especially those of us who are untrained, as the Roman Catholics have known for centuries—and express the inexpressible? We all know, don't we, that old line about the music program of the local church being the seat of the War Department? Music gets the honor, I think, because frequently our only regularly employed staff people in the area of arts, more's the pity, are the musicians. And we recognize that opinions about musical matters in the congregation are very strong, even irrational.

I think this is not just because the musicians among us are an inflammatory crowd, though certainly there is such a thing as artistic temperament, but also because music, like the other arts, can have such *power* in our lives. All of us respond to at least some art forms, and when I use the word art or art forms, I am not talking just about those items displayed downtown in the Museum of Fine Arts or played in the symphony hall or performed on public TV, but those manifestations of sight and sound all around us in our homes, our businesses, our schools, hopefully our churches, without which we are simply not complete human beings. One does not have to be a singer to enjoy Mozart or Pfautsch or Bernstein, or the unknown musician who wrote "Amazing Grace." One does not have to be a painter to respond to a Remington or a Rouault or a Bywaters, nor an architect to feel one's heart skip a beat as one enters Perkins Chapel on a late winter afternoon and sees those chandeliers sparkling with reflections of the setting sun as the light peeks through those wonderful clear glass windows.

Yes, we can live without beauty, and I can live without an arm or a leg, but not *wholly*—spell that any way you will. Who, then, will be responsible for the beautiful, for the arts?—especially that art that suggests the beauty of holiness, the sense of awe among us as we worship, something akin to what the scriptures mean, I think, when they say the fear of the Lord? Who, if not we Levites and priests, those who are responsible for the temple and what happens within it, with our staffs, our worship commissions, our choirs and actors and dancers, banner-makers, liturgists, architects. If we don't, who will? And what, in concrete terms, can we do to help restore mystery and reverence to our worship?

Surely a part of the task at least must be to take a look at some of the fine arts and see how we can use them regularly and comfortably in our services.

In the worship space itself, for instance: to what should we be sensitive? Truth, our architect friend Sövik says, is conveyed by honesty. Could not that mean the use of real live materials and letting them show?—real stone, real wood, letting that be itself instead of using fabricated imitations and hiding the real thing? Couldn't it mean, among other things, letting some of the organ pipes show, not stuffing them into some chamber and covering the chamber with scrim? Could it even mean using real flowers and shrubs instead of those plastic ones?

For Mr. Sövik, love is shown forth by hospitality: a room shaped and furnished in such a way that people are aware of one another and their dependence on one another, a room full of warm colors, windows, visuals, altar pieces, paraments, and vestments, a room that welcomes and does not intimidate. This is the reason, of course, for our recent love affair with semi-circular shapes, occurring as they do, sometimes in square or rectangular buildings like the one I worship in, that allow the congregation to be closer to one another and see each others' faces. Maybe our fan-shaped Akron plan had something! Whatever the attributes of the Gothic nave—that long, rectangular room with the center aisle and the congregation divided in the two blocks on either side—one does have to say that the message of the room when the chairs are put into it is that one literally must turn one's back on one's neighbor in order to face the altar.

Another ally waiting to be appreciated and used in the same search, I think, is drama. Indeed, the ties between drama and worship are so close that I suspect that, like Poe's readers searching for the purloined letter, we are likely to overlook it. The worship itself is drama, is it not? As most ritual is the acting out regularly and repetitively of certain basic understandings, that drama we act out every Sunday morning at 11 o'clock, regardless of how we spell it out, is our most fundamental one. It is *the* ultimate one, the drama of our very existence under God, of God's mighty act of salvation and our response to it. It is to this sacred place each week that we bring our broken and finite selves, pressured as they are, into the Almighty Presence, in the company of fellow pilgrims: to seek God's pardon and power, to hear the good news of God's redemption proclaimed, to become aware of God's forgiveness and enabling spirit, and to act out our grateful thanks in commitment to serve. One can hardly improve on the great model of Isaiah's sixth chapter, complete as it is with those three mighty acts of confession, proclamation, and dedication. This is what we understand our Sunday morning service to be, whether or not we put it down in liturgical terms on the bulletin; deep down, we know that it is just possible that in the midst of these actions in which we all participate as players the great God will indeed rend the heavens and come down, a member of the cast, even the lead player in the drama. This and our response to it is what the church is all about in worship. It is so potent, this drama, so close to us, so much a reality involving our whole selves, it is literally too deep for words. And yet, it is words, words, words, spoken and sung, that we use most often to try to express it.

I often think that the most wonderful thing that could happen to choirs in rehearsal would be for the conductor to come down with a genuine, four-star case of laryngitis and not be able to speak a word. One wonders what would happen to those of us responsible for leading public worship if we caught the bug, too, and had to fall back on some other means of communication in the service than human speech. We might be surprised then at the power of dramatic action. Even our playbill, our printed order, is frequently more of a kind of menu, or list of events that we intend to serve up to a congregation of more passive auditors than active members of the cast, listening to words spoken to them by someone else.

Though reading the scripture is fundamental to our lives and liturgy, for instance, frequently what we read is only a few verses from one book of the Bible. Occasionally we even may have the congregation recite a psalm from the psalter. (But I remind you that even the psalter has been abridged.)

Nehemiah's ceremony, without question, is high drama. The act of confession, for instance, is not only words but truly action. The people show up in sackcloth, with earth upon their heads. And when they bow their heads, the account says, they really bow, with their faces to the ground. The *Torah* is carefully placed in the position of honor and prominence, above the people, on a platform specially constructed for it, facing the water gate—an honorable location. When the priest opens the book, the people stand. When he blesses the Lord, they shout, "Amen, amen!" And when he reads from it, they weep. And does he read? From early morning to midday! Now that is a lot of reading and a lot of weeping, and the sermon hasn't even started yet. The sermon itself is the good news of God's love and care for his people, even their deliverance from bondage in spite of themselves. Their response is naturally thanksgiving, and they weep with joy, swearing an oath that they will give themselves and their first fruits to God's service and the maintenance of God's house. But they do more than that; it's more than just words. They take portions of that feast to those who have none. Expressions of truth and love and awe are not left to words alone, nor to the voice of the priest and Levites alone. They are acted out, at least symbolically. One's body is put on the line by everyone in attendance. Don't we get some sense of their awareness of the holy, of mystery, as we see the loving attention given to the dramatic details of worship in Israel? The whole event is carefully staged and choreographed, with movements and actions and words that suggest that something sacred is present here and something important is about to be done and said about it.

Many of you at one time participated in services where one of our resident liturgical dancers, Jerry Bywaters Cochran, danced the Word. You will remember that occasionally she danced a great hymn of Paul Gerhardt, (whom Bonhoeffer loved so much, you recall) "Awake My Heart," in which, when she came to the place where the text affirms "thy word my nurture," she went to the lectern, picked up the immense pulpit Bible, carried it to the altar table, held it high, and then let it drop with an enormous explosion on the table—a vivid non-verbal portrayal of the tremendous weight that that Word carries in our lives. Now certainly we do not expect to dance the Word every Sunday literally, but surely we can place that book in an honored, highly visible place, approach it with reverent steps (and teach our readers to do so), read from it with sure, steady, well-rehearsed voices, and thereby dramatize the fact in no uncertain or perfunctory terms that this Word indeed *is* our nurture, our very life, so that when the lesson is ended and the reader says, "Thus ends the reading," or "This is the Word of God," we can all gratefully respond, truly, with our "Amen, amen" or our "Thanks to be God" and really mean it.

Drama has to do not only with the content of the liturgy—what we do—but with the form of it as well—how we do it. The thoughtful arrangement of the service, the movements that reverently and clearly express the mood and content of what we are about, the timing and flow, the contrast between prayer and praise, between sense and reason, our insistence on clarity of things seen and heard—all of this takes study, preparation, and practice, practice, practice. Why should choir members be the only ones we expect to practice?

Talented laypeople, I think, are waiting in the wings of our congregations to be used as readers and liturgists and worship helpers—as Levites, if you will, and we have in our United Methodist Church a growing treasury of fine resource material to help us.

The Christian year itself is our heritage from history, reinforcing as it does on a seasonal scale what we do in our three acts of confession, proclamation, and dedication on any given Sunday. Advent, Christmas, and Epiphany in the winter cycle reflect these acts with all their colors and symbols, and Lent, Easter, and Pentecost do it all over again in the spring, with appropriate music and other art forms to bring it all to life. This is the great cosmic drama of our own lives under God. Surely such a drama requires no less serious planning and execution, and yes, performance, than an *Oedipus Rex* or a *Hamlet* or a *Death of a Salesman* or even of our children's and youths' productions of *David and the Giants* or *Lightshine*. The lectionary, with its systematic, balanced cycle of scripture readings, is constructed to incorporate the proclamation of the Word into this dramatic scheme, so it too becomes a useful dramatic form.

And what of music? Like all the other arts, doesn't it help us express the holy? I think it probably is the art form most familiar to us, the one that we seem most willing and ready to employ in the services of worship. Does it too speak with honesty, hospitality, and beauty, of truth, love, and mystery?

I must say that, as a Levite still trying after all these years to get her harp and a cymbal in tune, I can only answer that question, "Sometimes." For of all the artists in the service of the temple, I think it is we musician-Levites who have been the most reckless with the raw materials of ecstasy, perhaps because we use them so much. For instance, we have not always shown forth the truth fully. Like our architect brothers and sisters we have not always used honest materials, but simply imitations of what we know to be beautiful, or we have kept hidden what we should have revealed because we were afraid somebody wouldn't like it. We have also failed frequently in hospitality, as well. For we have limited our art to the performance by a few or to repertoire that speaks only to certain groups in the congregation, either to those whose taste on the one hand runs to the gospel style or to those whose taste on the other hand runs to the music of the Renaissance and before, or we have considered our own tastes to be superior rather than different. Furthermore, we have acted on occasion like an isolated elite, because we have forgotten that the heart of Christian worship in song is the hymnody of our people, not simply our choirs' repertory of anthems, no matter how fine that is.

But *sometimes* our music speaks appropriately. There is evidence that the state of this art in our worship is improving and becoming more effective in the service of the gospel. The numbers of committed, talented young people coming into this field are increasing, and more churches are putting them to work after graduation because they are giving their art and other arts high priority.

Aware of this, we would almost be tempted to believe that all is well in the choir lofts of Zion if it were not so obvious that we have a long,

long way to go. For though some of our music speaks the truth and some of it portrays love, too little of it these days suggests mystery. Did we in our adolescent 60s and 70s become so enamored of the folk style, for instance, with our guitars and our pop tunes, and so quickly seduced by the instant approval that this brought us that we never grew beyond that style and sound—never realized it could become so down-to-earth that it would lead us away from heavenly mystery? Did we concentrate on the human, even as we sang evangelical words, at the expense of the divine in our art? *Did we exaggerate hospitality at the expense of mystery?*

Much of the responsibility for that all-too-rarely sensed element of the holy is ours, I am afraid. Never did Levites need priests so desperately as in this area, where our music programs are intended to enrich and enhance our worship but where all too often they merely reflect the popular culture around us. We need you, preachers, to teach, suggest, and lead us Levite musicians to know better what liturgy is and how this art can serve liturgy better.

So we Levites say to you, our pastors and preachers: We have our service music. Show us how to fit it with the lectionary—with scripture and with sermon, not just to affirm what we are supposed to have learned from books in graduate school, but to demonstrate to us truly that in the real and lively local church the gospel can speak through our Halleluias and our Kyries and our Praise-the-Lords and the holy be somehow expressed in their beauty.

We have our anthems and our solos; teach us when and where to use them so that what we sing are not just "specials" but integral parts of a proclamation that is special and holy.

We have our psalms; insist that we remember that they are the songbook of all the people, not just of a few, and help us to find ways to make them once again the lively and lovely responses of the whole Church to the holy.

We have our organs, our strings and drums and bells; advise us how best to build and arrange the rooms we play them in, so that their notes and rhythms are not only music to our ears, but in deeper reverence, praise.

And we have our hymnals—old, new, and still to come; demand of us that we explore fully their treasure of poetry and tunes, familiar and unfamiliar, so that we can join each other in expressing through them the praise and prayer that wells up in us all, and so too that we can feel a part of that larger communion of saints who throughout the ages have sung their faith, discovering indeed that sometimes a light does surprise Christians while they sing!—a light that is holy.

As we ask this of you priests, we Levites who care for the temples where we worship, who bring all our arts into the service of the Word proclaimed within those temples, know that none of us can hear without a preacher. So above all else, open the book, read its words, and proclaim its Word to us, for without that central reality our ceremonial is empty and all our music and drama—our banners and paraments and dance and resounding sacred space—all of these are but sounding brass and tinkling cymbals, and we are but robot children playing church with artistic toys that are little more than momentary entertainment. Preach the Word to us and compel us to unite, like knowledge and vital piety, those two so long divided—art and reason, the sensory and the cerebral, the non-verbal and the verbal—so that together we priests and Levites may prepare a place and an occasion where devotion to truth, commitment to love, and an awareness of the presence of the Holy One—the essence of our religion—may be found. Preach the Word to us, proclaim its Gospel: and we will bow the knees of our hearts and shout, "Amen, amen!"

Can the Director Teach It?
Then Singers Can Sing It!

(Published in Choristers Guild LETTERS, May 1980)

People who sing together in church are generally good learners. I am struck by this fact again and again as I visit choirs and congregations and see how readily they respond in singing new and unfamiliar music.

I think I know some of the reasons. Music itself is pleasurable, and almost everyone responds agreeably to some form of it. Furthermore, the church is a community where people are already supportive of each other and reasonably unified in understanding and purpose; that unity and support make for an environment conducive to learning.

Such a happy state of affairs opens a world of possibilities to the music director who recognizes that a large part of the music a church is able to do depends on that director. For I am convinced *choirs and congregations can learn almost anything the director can teach them.* Good teaching is built on three foundation blocks: the learner's self-confidence, the learner's motivation, and the director's clarity in presenting the material.

Most directors know the importance of building self-confidence in a singing group and would agree, in fact, that very little learning can take place without it. Yet I think directors often downplay, even fail to recognize, the inadequacy non-musicians feel in the presence of musicians, professional or non-professional. Congregations feel this way about the choir, and many choir members feel this way about their choir director, often through no fault of anyone. The physical area where teaching goes on, in rehearsal room or sanctuary or chapel, hardly helps; for as Dr. Harris suggested in *I'm OK, You're OK* (Thomas A. Harris, M.D.; Harper and Row, 1967), the set-up of a room where the learners are seated together in front of a teacher who stands before them suggests an inferior-superior transaction before the material to be learned is even presented.

In any event, the first job the director-teacher has to do is to break down that feeling of inadequacy and build up the self-assurance of the singers.

I have never yet seen a choir or congregation that did not respond favorably to encouragement. This doesn't mean a teacher should overlook mistakes or pretend something sounds good when it does not. Singers usually know when they're wrong, and a director who doesn't honestly recognize and deal with their errors undermines their trust in short order. But it does mean heartily accentuating the positive and congratulating the group whenever there is reason to—indeed, it means finding reason to do so as often as possible. My conducting teacher always insisted that his students point out specifically the strengths of the classmate up in front of the group conducting before they began analyzing weaknesses, and I've found that to be a most productive practice. There are always strengths: an easy smile, appropriate tension, an expressive legato beat, and the like. Mentioning these strengths by name helps build confidence, the indispensable ingredient in every successful conductor, and makes one more secure and ready to analyze and improve one's technique.

Singers respond similarly.

Confidence-building means smiling often, especially when things go wrong early in the learning process. It means being willing to acknowledge one's own conducting errors openly. Making choral music is a shared experience where everyone, director included, is in the enterprise together for the enrichment of all concerned, performers and listeners alike; nothing contributes more to that sharing than the director's ability to convey the idea, without sacrificing any leadership qualities, that he or she is part of the team, too.

Motivation, or wanting to sing, is boosted considerably by those factors identified earlier—that music is by and large pleasurable and that the church is an environment friendly to learning. But we all know that not every potential singer in choir or congregation would choose to sing every song the director presents at the time designated for it. Personalities, taste, backgrounds, and conditions differ, and it is a richer and more fascinating world because that is so.

What, then, motivates a congregation to sing a new hymn or the choir a new anthem—or even an old one they may not particularly like? A lot of things: duty, habit, group pressure, pride, respect for authority, appreciation of the text or tune, some understanding of its appropriateness to the service. All these can be encouraged and used profitably in teaching.

But nothing can beat pure pleasure as a motivating impulse—the anticipation of making musical sounds together because it is fun.

Conveying that feeling takes preparation, too. A director has ongoing homework: to listen continually to music of all kinds—in concert and on recordings, on radio and television, and to explore new hymnbooks and read good literature, all of which will expand musical, literary, and spiritual horizons and thereby increase one's own capacity for enjoyment. Sometimes a song is appealing primarily because of its melody, sometimes because of its rhythmic patterns, or its harmony, its texture, its counterpoint, its tonal colors, its form, or its words. A director who is constantly listening for these musical elements increases his or her own delight in a wide variety of sounds and is thereby better able to teach with an infectious enthusiasm. One thing is certain: motivating a group to try a new song that holds no interest for the director is all but impossible.

Besides preparation and enthusiasm are a smile, a welcoming attitude toward the singers that will invite their participation rather than demand it, a steadfast resolve not to scold or threaten, and above all a secure control over the desire to talk too much. Overdoing verbal instructions, or inserting spoken words into the singing, or stopping the music to say something can kill motivation cold.

Presenting the song effectively will combine confidence-building and good motivation with other specific techniques that set out the music to be learned as clearly and quickly as possible. Often the best teaching is no teaching, namely, letting the choir or congregation discover the music for themselves.

In teaching a round, say the *Tallis Canon*, to a congregation, the procedure could go something like this:

Without verbal introduction or any accompaniment (throughout), the director sings the melody, with the words, several times alone, eventually inviting, by gesture only, the people to join in, following the director's voice, words, and hand motions suggesting the rise and fall of pitches. Gradually the director eliminates the "crutches"—the hand motions, mouthing of words, and singing—so the group members are singing comfortably on their own. Only then will they be secure enough to risk following the director's gesture indicating the melody is to be sung in two-part canon. When the two-part singing is confident, the leader can signal the division of the group into four parts and cue the entrance of each part so a four-part round results. (Where this hymntune appears in hymnals, it usually includes the "Doxology" words often sung to OLD 100TH, so memorizing text is not a problem.) By the time all these steps have been completed, the melody has been sung at least a dozen times and should be firmly installed in the singers' memories. No words ever need be spoken at any point by the director. An "Amen" in parts can be indicated by mouthing and gesture at the close, since "Amen" is historically appropriate after a doxological stanza.

Many variations of the process exist, of course. A hymn that the singers can look at as they hear it can be played on piano or organ with fully harmonized accompaniment, provided the melody is prominent. Hymns like "Holy Spirit, Truth Divine" set to CANTERBURY, in which the harmony is rich, appealing, and absolutely basic (here's where the director's musical understanding comes in) should be introduced this way, not simply a melodic line. Hearing the lovely harmony is part of the fun and makes the singing easier. It is not necessary, of course, to repeat the tune as often when an accompanying instrument is used.

It is important, also, to let the group hear the hymn the first few times all the way through. After that, non-musicians can usually learn best by dealing with phrases cumulatively.

I follow this idea in introducing a new anthem to a choir, letting them read it all the way through the first time at the indicated tempo, with accompaniment, free to discover the perils and pleasures of the score themselves. Nothing is more frustrating to singers than to be stopped by the director and made to rehearse a small spot before they've had a chance to become acquainted with the whole anthem into which the parts must be made to fit. Other conductors accomplish this overview successfully by asking their singers to mark their scores, noting repeated contrasting sections before they sing the piece. No one method is sacred, only the principle. If it works and is musical and practical, do it!

The attitude of the director is always vitally important: friendly, positive, relaxed, and understanding, but with techniques clear, precise, and compelling. Sharpening attitudes and skills takes careful study and practice ahead of time by both the director and the accompanist. If additional instruments like handbells or drums are called for, they are best rehearsed separately, then added to the ensemble after the chorus is secure with the work.

The director in all of the phases of the learning process is the key, and a well-taught group can handle almost any material. A director who chooses appropriate music for choir and congregation can make the singing of it not only a delightful musical experience, but a worshipful one as well.

Tradition and Spontaneity

(© The Liturgical Conference, 1017 12th St. NW, Washington, DC 20005. All rights reserved. Used with permission.)

A community freshens and clarifies its life story by regularly taking time for remembering, for structuring the past in a way that has meaning for today. Thus tradition, suggesting time past, is established and assimilated, particularly when it is dramatized and ritualized in liturgies. Spontaneity, suggesting time present, also enters the process as each local community retells its story, bringing diversity, apparent unpredictability, and surprise into the liturgy.

Not so long ago, we didn't talk much about the contrasting qualities of tradition and spontaneity because we were not reflective about worship. Service on the Lord's Day, usually referred to in my Presbyterian childhood as Sunday morning church, followed an unchanging order from week to week. Little variation occurred even in the parish announcements or the familiar hymns and responses sung by the choir. The structure of our midweek prayer meeting and the "opening exercises" of Sunday school also remained constant.

It did not occur to us youngsters or to most of our elders to question the repetition of these forms, nor to wonder why we had no lay worship committee to work with the pastor to study and plan services. In fact, if one defines liturgy literally as "the work of the people," one would have been hard pressed to find much liturgy in our services. The worship service was something done to or for us, not by us (unless we sang in the choir); it was an exercise planned and carried out almost entirely by the clergy.

Predictable and holy

Bible-belt Presbyterians celebrated two high holy days, Christmas and Easter. The high moments of our observance of the former were reserved for the Santa Claus party in the fellowship hall, at which the old man himself gave bags of candy and oranges to the kids. As for Easter, the climax of the celebration occurred at the sunrise service in which the young people re-enacted the visit of the women to the empty tomb. The form and mood of the regular services for these days, however, duplicated all the other services of the year. Only in the "extra" events of party and pageant did we catch the flavor of celebration or awe appropriate to those great feasts.

Most of us, in short, were comfortable with our corporate rituals, content to accept their predictability from week to week and year to year. Tradition was strong and almost totally governed our worship, though our understanding of it was minimal. If we had been asked about the meaning of tradition, we would have answered in denominational terms: "Baptists immerse, Episcopalians chant, and Roman Catholics pray in Latin." Routine more than tradition, and practice more than creed identified us, even to ourselves.

Unless we had been involved in the fundamentalist-liberal controversy that surfaced in some churches during the '20s and '30s, we knew little about the formative events that shaped our denomination. Our knowledge of history remained confined chiefly to our local congregation; few of us knew anything about the church's Jewish and early Christian roots, the heroic women and men of faith in ages past, or why we did what we did in our liturgies. That information was consigned to textbooks used by pastors in their seminary days. We did not know how such information related to the real world of praise and prayer. Whatever church history or theology we might have been exposed to originated in the church education rooms and more often than not stayed there, only minimally informing what we did in the sanctuary. Certainly we were not aware of a connection.

The power of repeated action

To say that we were unreflective about tradition during the first half of this century is not to minimize the tradition's importance; it is, rather, to affirm its power. However little we grasped this power, it was definitely a force shaping our lives and worship. Originating as belief, it was transmitted through unvarying repetition and habit in our practice, so that eventually the practice itself became tradition. We know this to be true even today: the style, order, sounds, and gestures of liturgy remain in the bone and bloodstream of the worshiping community long after the beliefs that gave birth to them have slipped into storage. Some among us may know the centuries-old history of our ritual actions, but there are great numbers of us—particularly those who are young in the faith, regardless of chronological age—who simply know the actions. The actions still define us most clearly.

William Holmes, a former pastor of my church, used to illustrate this kind of identity-building by describing the festival dances of the native American tribes he watched as a tourist in Gallup, New Mexico. The men of the tribe, he said, gathered in an inner circle to dance, while the wives and young children arranged themselves in an outer circle as onlookers. But as the dancing progressed and the excitement mounted, the children edged closer and closer, drawn as if by a magnet into the inner circle. They fell in behind their fathers, mimicked their gestures, and became part of the dance themselves. They were not aware of the rationale for the ceremony or the dance; that would come later. Yet they experienced the ritual's mood and power expressed by moving bodies swaying to insistent drums, and they identified with it by joyfully joining in.

Actions truly speak louder than words in liturgical practice. Yet if actions are not eventually informed by the theological understanding they are designed to express, and if they are retained solely because of their familiarity, they can lose their focus. They may even begin to represent other beliefs far afield from those originally intended and professed.

One summer Sunday I visited a church in my neighborhood that had recently built a beautiful new sanctuary, complete with a fine organ. I knew that this church followed a liturgical form meaningful to me. As the ritual unfolded, I became aware that few people were singing the hymns or otherwise participating in more than a halfhearted and perfunctory way, but I blamed this on unfortunately dry acoustics and summertime in general. I assumed things would perk up when the offering was presented at the altar and the familiar "Old Hundredth" doxology was intoned.

I was wrong. That action and its attendant singing were as dispirited and weak as the previous events had been. Not until the acolytes brought forward the American flag (leaving the Christian flag behind) and the organ and congregation shifted into the final stanza of "America" did the mood change and the room come alive. As a visiting outsider, I had no idea why this was so, but the actions of this community telegraphed a signal to me that was not at all representative of the creed they professed.

The return of spontaneity

Even though they understand tradition poorly and variously, a majority of worshipers nevertheless recognize it as an essential ingredient of their corporate life. Some might debate the forms it takes and the practices that attempt to express it with varying degrees of success, but almost all would agree that tradition is vital. Spontaneity is another matter, however. Except in liturgies that invited extemporaneous prayers and responses or lay witness (i.e., Quaker meeting, the black church, some sects), spontaneity was a missing quality in North American liturgical practice during the first half of this century.

One can affirm this absence, I think, whether one thinks of spontaneity as the unpredictable and unplanned event or in the broader sense as freshness, difference, change, the quality of the new in an event. As I think back on my own Presbyterian-Methodist history, I see a very narrow version of spontaneity surfacing primarily in the form of sentence prayers offered in prayer meetings or youth groups. I can recall little that was extemporaneous in the Sunday service, however. Inviting members of the congregation to voice prayers of joy or concern in that setting would not have occurred to us. Nor did we think of introducing dance or the other arts into the service to enliven it, or of forming lay-clergy teams to plan worship creatively and give it at least a feeling of spontaneity—these were definitely ideas whose time had not yet come.

Their time did come, of course, after World War II, and it came quickly, impelled by theological renewal movements and the explosion in communications hinted at earlier by the invention of the radio. The renewal movements, developing out of forces that had been brewing during the '30s in Europe, were symbolized and focused in Vatican II. These movements primarily affected the religious community; however, the revolution in communications affected everybody, as Marshall McLuhan and James White have pointed out. [See Marshall McLuhan, *Understanding Media: The Extensions of Man* (New York: New American Library, Signet Books, 1966); James F. White, *New Forms of Worship* (Nashville, Tennessee: Abingdon Press, 1971).]

Television, with its power to set the viewer in the midst of world events as they happen, came into virtually every North American home. The world was very much with us, a world changing so fast that news dependent on the printed page was out of date by the time the page was distributed. Television and radio gave us front-row seats at catastrophes occurring all over the world. Can anyone forget the sight of starving African children or of a president gunned down on a Texas street? The new media produced a new strain of North Americans, whose understanding of life around them was conditioned by their response to what they saw unfolding on the television screen at that second. In such an environment, traditional worship patterns were bound to change if they were to connect at all with the rest of life.

Worshipers raised in this environment demanded a new kind of liturgy. James White comments on this situation:

> This new communications revolution has happened to us so fast that we are hardly aware of its effects on us. We still judge it in terms of our past, putting movies on television just as we made movies out of books. Yet the great importance of what television (along with the telephone, speed in travel, and other new possibilities) has done for us

is often ignored when it is seen just as an alternate way of presenting the same information. That is to miss the point altogether. Marshall McLuhan has argued that the medium itself is the message and we must perceive what the new media do to us, not just the message they present. Our thesis here is that the new media, especially television, have caused a drastic change in our means of perceiving reality, just as the advent of mass literacy did in the sixteenth century....It is as if we all once again were squatted around a tribal campfire, taking part in whatever was happening to the tribe. But that tribe is now world-wide. Instead of the perimeter of the village campfire being our widest horizon, we now find ourselves elbow to elbow with the whole human race. (White, *New Forms of Worship*, p. 29.)

The reality of the modern world, then, makes it imperative that we bring the spontaneity of the present and the tradition that was the past together into some sort of meaningful ritual.

Experimenting with new ways

In some parishes, ministers sensitive to this demand, influenced by revitalized biblical and theological study and aware of the need for an adequately expressive liturgy, began searching for new and more dramatic ways to present old truths. They experimented with previously untried methods of encouraging the people's response. In other congregations, lay members who had read Tillich, Maritain, Bonhoeffer, and the existentialists caught the spirit and pressed their clergy into the same search. Still other laypeople and clergy, alarmed and burdened by cataclysmic eruptions in the culture, found traditional worship wanting and turned to movements emphasizing a freer, more individualistic, sometimes charismatic style—a style soon welcomed by television for mass consumption.

In the mainline Protestant and Catholic denominations in the United States worship planning committees sprang up; banners, dance, drama, and other art forms appeared in worship services; new liturgies emerged, often unique to a local congregation, and ancient practices—the passing of the peace, for example—were revived for the first time in centuries. The guitar, so expressive of the anguish of a generation emotionally and physically dismembered by the Korean and Vietnamese conflicts, entered the sanctuary, bringing intimacy and informality. More important, laypeople began to plan and execute Sunday services, thus recovering what had been theirs from the start—the liturgy, the "work of the people." Spontaneity, in the form of creativity and lay involvement, came back to the church.

What happened then, and is still happening, is well documented. It always happens when the windows are thrown open in a room kept airtight for a long time. Fresh air blows in, bringing with it a bit of dust and a few bugs. Like tradition in liturgy, creativity and freedom carry dangers as well as blessings, and many congregations of the '60s and '70s, while accepting the changes, quickly became aware of the dangers. Others, slower to alter traditional forms or practices, are only now identifying the perils: too much change too fast for the congregation to absorb; focus on personnel rather than on content; preoccupation with a single style to the neglect of others (one thinks of all the "folk" songs and anthems that, while good in themselves, crowded out good literature of other kinds); acceptance of practices of questionable quality, and actions and events created without an understanding of what James White calls the theological, historical, or pastoral rationale necessary to keep them responsible. (White, *New Forms of Worship*, p. 32.) These are just a few of the difficulties that continue to challenge liturgy planners.

A new partnership

Even so, tradition has been joined by spontaneity on the liturgical scene, and it is likely that the two principles will remain together. The last two decades have seen a fair amount of struggle in the marriage, with one partner seeking now and again to dominate the other. Margaret Mead viewed attempts to abandon traditional forms during this period with a sharp eye:

> In the 1970s, young people have been demanding more life and color, more contemporaneousness in their lives; they have responded to this depreciation of existing ceremonial and to the belief that ritual is bad by trying to invent absolutely new things—"happenings"—with form and content completely unpredictable and new. But each of these inventions has become stylized, stereotyped, repetitive, and boring to those who perform and those who watch. The shallowness of a tradition of complete improvisation and absolute lack of predictability lacks the essential elements of great celebrations in which tried forms, polished by years of loving use, are infused with new life, ritualistic events which can be enjoyed just because the forms themselves or the content are familiar.
>
> One ability that man lacks—at least as far as he has now

evolved—is the ability to invent continually something entirely new. Real innovation is rare and inexpressibly precious, set as it always is within a rich and productive legacy from the past, or a shared view of the present or the future. And if the greatly original artist has to create the kind of tradition on which other artists are able to draw, too much energy goes into such forms. Endless (and invariably mediocre) innovation is far more stereotyped than traditional form; we end up not with miracle plays or Verdi or Gilbert and Sullivan but with the themes of grade B movies and soap operas. One mediocrity cannot be distinguished from another, as each insists on being different with a genre too feeble to nourish any real originality. [Margaret Mead, *Twentieth Century Faith: Hope and Survival* (Harper & Row Publishers, 1972).]

Despite all the progress, the tension between tradition and spontaneity remains very much with us. A few congregations that have followed the same order of worship for a long time have managed to close ranks behind tradition, resisting all but the most minimal changes; for them, change itself is the enemy. Even in churches and temples where a more innovative or spontaneous style has emerged, some worshipers are uncomfortable with the new expressions, whether they say so or not. Creativity is still feeling its way into a permanent relationship with tradition, and progress advances at an uneven pace. The balloons and confetti that helped awaken some congregations have for the most part disappeared, but they made their point, and they gave many fledgling worship committees courage. These groups found that, indeed, they could not come up with something new every Sunday, but neither could they return to a style of liturgy that never varied.

I remember one Methodist minister, who, after having served several older churches, was very careful in his latest appointment not to change anything. He was greatly perplexed when he began to hear the frequent complaint, "We always do everything exactly the same way every Sunday!" New forms and events can stimulate an interest in their content and even in the belief behind them, so that many congregations begin to appreciate their tradition more than ever before. They realize that old and new must work in tandem, each complementing the other, for liturgical expression to be complete. Margaret Mead suggests that an appreciation for the old is a necessary groundwork for the new:

> When we look at traditional societies—like Bali, for example—we find that celebration is inseparable from ritual. Highly stylized activities, repeated from celebration to celebration, from procession to procession, from year to

year, are an essential part of the whole. Large events may allow ample room for new elements, new songs, new drama, new costumes, new skits on the current world, but nevertheless the element of ritual, of sanctioned and valued repetition, is always there. Improvisation is possible because it can be done within a known and valued frame. [Margaret Mead, *Twentieth Century Faith: Hope and Survival* (New York: Harper & Row Publishers, 1972).]

Challenges for worship planners

The main task now is to find methods that accomplish the union of old and new, requiring no small measure of teaching, pastoral sensitivity, and skill. Those planning services must first know their own tradition and people in order to make new practices welcome—prayers, acclamations, songs, dances, dramatic events, contemporary readings, visual arts, and silences.

Erik Routley used to remind church musicians that they had no greater obligation or challenge than to take the music they knew to be beautiful and worthy and make it "friendly" to congregations that had little musical expertise. Those who knew Routley recognized that by "beautiful and worthy" he meant hymns, anthems, and organ music of proven quality, whatever their style or age. He would never compromise on the integrity of the material he chose to teach, but he had a delightful way of making congregations feel comfortable with the new hymns and antiphons he wanted them to learn.

In order to make a start, worship planning groups first need to educate themselves in a solid understanding of the scriptures, church history, theology, and liturgics. Only then will the services they plan communicate to the congregation the real nature of the church's tradition and appropriate ways to participate in its liturgical expression. Some groups schedule this kind of instruction into their regular meetings; others offer it in special sessions convened for the purpose. Parish clergy, ministers from other churches, or visiting lecturers from a nearby seminary or university can often supply the necessary background and preparation.

The liturgy planning group may also be able to encourage the parish education staff or committee to make such information available to larger segments of the church membership. Together they can develop curricula for church school classes for all age groups and for adult and children's choir sessions. Symbolism, church architecture, liturgical arts, hymnody, and church history are subjects that many church members know little about but find fascinating. The more congregations learn about these matters, the more meaning they discover in the drama of worship.

Those working in liturgy also need to help the music director of the church make hymn-singing more frequent and enjoyable. The North American church is in the midst of a renaissance in hymnody, with almost every one of its major religious bodies having just completed, or at least begun work on, a new hymnal. Provision for teaching new hymns (and relishing old ones of all styles) needs attention, for the Sunday service alone cannot acquaint a congregation with the huge volume of exciting, rich material from its own and other traditions now coming into print. Hymn-sings are called for, and so are acoustically live rooms in which to hold them. In the United States, carpeting and soundproofing have robbed sanctuaries of the "ring" that makes community participation rewarding. Liturgy committees might well undertake a study of acoustics and the theological understanding of the church that must necessarily inform its application to worship spaces.

Worship planners must also make provision for coaching and training those who are to take part in the liturgical drama. Not only acolytes, but all who take any leadership role in the service must be chosen and instructed well. The best idea in the world can be sabotaged in two minutes by poor execution, and no committee should assume that their assignments will be carried out as conceived without rehearsal. Lay readers also need to be coached in voice production, projection, timing, and pronunciation. Nearly every congregation includes a speech teacher who can be recruited to meet with readers each week and practice the lessons. Ushers also need training, and those who help with communion or other ceremonies must be instructed regularly.

Sometimes churches that have not had a liturgy committee before have introduced new elements into their services by concentrating on a few of the festive seasons or days in the church's tradition, like Easter, Advent, and Christmas. More than once, a clergy-lay ad hoc planning committee organized for such a special celebration has turned into a permanent group with a rotating membership, ready to work with the clergy and other staff in planning worship on a regular basis.

One church in my area set up this type of special task force to plan a festival Pentecost service and fine arts week that included a display of paintings and sculptures done by church members and local artists. The event was such a success and so effective as an expression of Spirit-filled creation that the task force became a permanent fine arts committee. The more people are involved in serious planning under the right leadership, the more interest is generated in corporate experiences in a liturgical framework.

These are some of the concerns that occupy the time and energy of laity and clergy as they seek methods for blending spontaneity and tradition. Much more remains to be explored—so much, in fact, that those who want to move more quickly than others in the search can easily become discouraged. When frustration sets in, it may be well to remember that such an enterprise has never been easy or speedy. Our model always remains the incarnation: when the Word became flesh, it brought with it surprise, action, threat, and infinite possibilities for life. All this is still happening, as the Word becomes flesh in our own communities. No matter how deeply liturgy committees feel the weight of responsibility for making beautiful things happen in worship, it is still the Spirit that blows gracefully through our endeavors.

Teachers in the Church's Future

(Reprinted from Music Ministry, May 1978. Copyright © 1978 by Graded Press, The United Methodist Publishing House, Nashville, TN. Used by permission.)

In a panel discussion at the "Horizons 77" convocation I made a statement that got me into trouble with some strangers who don't know me and some friends who do.

"The days of regimented, vested children's choirs as we have known them," I said, "are numbered."

Taken by itself, that is a bald, negative statement. And when it showed up as a headline in Methodist news service reports afterward without the rest of the discussion that went with it, it naturally caused some consternation among my colleagues who direct children's choirs.

But I will stick with my observation, so long as the whole, positive context from which it was lifted is stated with it. And that is this: Whatever the state of formal, vested children's choirs trained exclusively for performance in occasional Sunday services, the song of children (and adults) is not dead in the church, not by a long shot. At least, it need not be. If it is, it is because we are missing opportunities that are in fact opening to us on every hand as the church moves into the future. Finding and using these opportunities to the full means being increasingly attentive to our primary role in the church, the role of educator.

The choir director's growing responsibility as educator—that, in a nutshell, was what that discussion was about, and I think it has direct implications for the future of music in the church. This is not a new subject. Carlton Young, editor of the *United Methodist Hymnal*, has said the same thing better and sooner, and others have echoed him. But I think it needs saying repeatedly.

The profile of tomorrow's church, which demands that its choir directors take more seriously their teaching role, begins to emerge looking something like this:

—It will be a church whose worship forms are more carefully thought out but whose worship style is freer, the planning and execution of which are shared by clergy and laity of both sexes and several races working together.

—It will be a church in which the emphasis of the liturgy is not so much on something new or something old but on a blending of the two, and the scriptures will be the liturgy's centerpiece.

—It will be a church in which sermons may frequently take nonverbal forms, using the arts in multi-media techniques, and in which more care is given to the room in which worship happens—its shape, its proper sound, its colors, and texture.

—It will be a church in which day-care, day schools, mother's-day-out programs, and continuing education for all ages keep the church buildings more efficiently filled through the week.

—It will be a church in which congregations increasingly find their mission outside the church's walls, in person-to-person and group-to-group activities seen as the church at work in the world.

The profile can be fleshed out with all kinds of additional shadings, but by and large it will look something like this, I think, and soon. And it will represent a better balance of in-the-church activity and outside-the-church activity than we have known in a long time. It also will carry with it a trunkful of temptations, excess baggage about which the church always has known a great deal.

Where worship is concerned, for instance, the temptation will continue to be, as we search for community in an impersonal, technological society, to play up the human-to-human relationship to the neglect of the God-human-God dimension—in short, to become and remain folksy and casual in our handling of ritual and ceremonial. We need to do a lot of work here, and the choir director, who deals week in and week out with ritual and liturgy, is an obvious choice to assist the clergy in training congregations and worship planning groups in such matters.

Freedom always freights danger with it, of course, and Protestants would do well to watch how their Roman Catholic neighbors have conducted worship since the breezes of Vatican II reform began to blow through the chancels of both communions a few years ago. In such changes as using English and turning the priest to face the people during the Mass, many Romans learned to infuse their liturgical motions with a grace and style that managed to include the people without excluding God in God's mystery. Thereby they have achieved a balance in the creator-creature drama we call liturgy that communicates the Ultimate to the deepest recesses of the human heart. They are still searching for the appropriate music for their freer forms, a search that has built-in temptations of its own, but they will find it.

Protestants, however, since the latest reformation in worship, have been more vulnerable to the threat of anything-goes folksiness in their services, especially in churches with a non-liturgical format. Lacking the sense of mystery and awe that the Mass and the Christian year create, they (we) have used this freedom to add not the warmth of the human touch to the mystery but rather an it's-OK-if-we're-all-involved informality to what was already a pretty cozy style. Church musicians who know something about the arts and their place in worship more and more will need to sharpen their teaching techniques to help congregations appropriate art forms tastefully, even as they learn from pastors something of the theology and history of worship. Where clergy and musician do not share the same understanding on such matters, both must assume the role of educator and find ways to learn together. The whole business of sight and sound in the sanctuary—the use of banners and paraments bearing Christian symbols and pipe organs requiring proper acoustics before installation—is an area crying for good teachers.

A new understanding of Christian education and mission, energy conservation, and economic pressures are combining, as Carlton Young says, to demand fuller and more efficient use of church buildings throughout the week and are thus helping close the gap between church and world. We are going to be looking into the Judeo-Christian heritage more seriously, I think, in an attempt to discover our roots; we are already recovering some responsible Bible-centered study. Diverse forces, a secular technological culture on the one hand and a fundamentalistic reaction to it on the other, are pushing us to the latter, and the pressure is not likely to abate but to intensify. Supreme Court rulings attempting to clarify the separation of church and state leave the way open for the church—with its already available facilities, curricula, and staff—to step into the educational vacuum.

Here I should point out that music in the public schools continues to be de-emphasized, especially at the elementary level. It may well be that in the very near future the only classroom where music is taught is in the church, not the public school. What was formerly the choir room where the children's choir rehearsed for a Thanksgiving service may in addition become the studio where Bach and Brahms and Britten are introduced and the tools of composition and music appreciation are shared. The church that finds a way to minister to the world—in the classroom, in retirement homes, downtown, in the ghetto, in hospitals—will probably make that way easier if it takes with it music, a small instrumental ensemble, singers, or youngsters using their own homemade instruments, along with their guitars and recorders. The possibilities are infinite.

What is clear is that we must be ready to move into every area of the church's life, not just as performers but as music teachers as well. Teaching is not all that new, of course, but basically what we have been doing all along. No choir director ever prepared a choir well to sing an anthem who did not employ every possible pedagogical skill. Teaching a congregation to sing a new response five minutes before the service or, harder still, within the service, is simply more of the same teaching practiced and sharpened to get the job done faster with greater numbers of people.

Good teaching does not just happen. It takes talent, study, and experience—all elements of good pedagogy. So does providing church school teachers with songs and hymns and other musical resources to complement their class work. So does encouraging new hymn writers, budding instrumentalists, potential pianists. So does educating a congregation to know music appropriate for weddings and funerals—*before* the need arises. So does conducting community-sings at church dinners or church retreats. And so, always, does preparing choirs to sing beautiful music well in the service of worship.

If the profile is anywhere near accurate, all this and more will be part of the musician's role as educator in the church of tomorrow, wherever making music can become a meaningful part of human experience. And no education is more basically "religious" than this. The choir director will still have the responsibility for getting an artistic performance from the church's choirs on Sunday; no one else is charged with or prepared for that function in the unique way the musician is. This expanded role simply means seeing that function as but one in a whole constellation of ministries that calls us to be educators. I believe the children's choir director, in particular, if in trying to organize a new group finds the takers fewer than in the past, need not despair and give up, but expect to find other ways within the church structure to reach children with music. The joyful noise will be there waiting for a wise and well-prepared teacher to coax it from the throats of highly motivated singers. We should not look for this music exclusively in the performing choir vested and in place in the chancel on Sunday morning, though that will remain the group uniquely prepared and committed to perform musical offerings of the highest quality in the service of worship.

Rhymes of Grace

Has Anybody Seen Christmas?

Has anybody seen Christmas
  underneath the glitter and the sequins and the bows?
    Anybody seen Christmas?

Look closer, look deep.
  Glitter's just the wrapping if love's the gift inside;
    so underneath the glitter may be Christmas.

Has anybody seen Christmas,
  lost among the parties and the chatter and the noise?
    Anybody seen Christmas?

Look closer, look deep.
  Often at a party a stranger finds a friend;
    so even in the parties may be Christmas.

Has anybody seen Christmas
  in the hurry and the rush, in the crowds and being tired?
    Anybody seen Christmas?

In all the time and trouble
  may be Christmas,
    may be a manger,
      may be a Baby,
        may be Love.

—Jane Marshall

© 1971 Hope Publishing Co., Carol Stream, IL 60188. All rights reserved.

Advent Prayer

(Previously unpublished)

God who made us,
God who loves us,
   now receive our Advent prayer.
Come refresh us,
come renew,
      restore your children everywhere.

To those hurting,
to those grieving
   sick in body, sick in soul,
Come with healing,
come with comfort,
      come, O God, and make them whole.

To those bored and
to those burdened,
   trudging down an endless road,
Come, bring meaning
to their living,
      come and lift their heavy load.

To those warring,
to those wanton,
   those who lust for pomp and power,
Come, convert them,
come, redeem them,
      rend the heavens, come down this hour.

To those righteous,
to those faithful,
   those who seek to walk your way,
Come, confirm them,
come, assure them,
      come impel them on today.

To us saints and
to us sinners—
    those whose hearts you know so well,
Come in judgment,
come in mercy,
    come, O come, Emmanuel.

—Jane Marshall

© 1992 Hope Publishing Co., Carol Stream, IL 60188. All rights reserved.

Advent People

(Previously unpublished)

Advent people, watch and hope;
  God will not delay.
God will bring the kingdom in;
  meanwhile, work and pray.

Advent people, watch and hope;
  strive for what is just.
God will make the crooked straight;
  meanwhile, work and trust.

Advent people, watch and hope;
  weep and laugh and share
bread with those you find in need.
  Till his coming, care.

Advent people, watch and hope;
  Christ that day will bring
freedom, wholeness, joy, and peace.
  Meanwhile, work and sing.

Advent people, watch and hope;
  God's good gift receive.
Now and Then are in God's hands;
  work and rest and live.

—Jane Marshall

© 1992 Hope Publishing Co., Carol Stream, IL 60188. All rights reserved.

Will We Find a Way?

Will we find a way to break away from hate?
   Good will and common sense can be a strong defense.
     Will we find a way?

Will we find a way to say a "nay" to war,
   to use our power and wealth for happiness and health?
     Will we find a way?

Will we find a way to put away the bomb,
   to blow away that cloud, that hellish mushroom cloud?
     Will we find a way?

Will we find a way to turn away from death,
   to take a brave new tack and cut the stockpiles back?
     Will we find a way?

Will we find a way to speed the day of peace,
   to learn what life's about before the time runs out?
     Will we find a way?

—Jane Marshall

© 1985 Hope Publishing Co., Carol Stream, IL 60188. All rights reserved.

What Gift Can We Bring?

What gift can we bring, what present, what token?
What words can convey it, the joy of this day?
When grateful we come, remembering, rejoicing,
    what song can we offer in honor and praise?

Give thanks for the past, for those who had vision,
who planted and watered so dreams could come true.
Give thanks for the now, for study, for worship,
    for mission that bids us turn prayer into deed.

Give thanks for tomorrow, full of surprises,
for knowing whatever tomorrow may bring,
we're given God's Word that always, forever,
    we rest in God's keeping and live in God's love.

—Jane Marshall

© 1982 Hope Publishing Co., Carol Stream, IL 60188. All rights reserved.

You Call Us, Lord

(Previously unpublished)

You call us, Lord, to be
a people set apart,
to feel with thoughtful mind
and think with tender heart.

Refrain:
Thus chosen, now, O Lord, we ask
for faith in your unfailing grace
to make us equal to the task.

You call us, Lord, to care
for self and neighbor, too,
to take the risk, and dare
to show what love can do. (Ref.)

You call us, Lord, to be
good stewards of the earth;
to tend it as a place
of blessedness and worth. (Ref.)

You call us, Lord, to serve:
to die that we may live,
to know we best receive
when joyfully we give. (Ref.)

May be sung to the trad. tune RHOSYMEDRE (66.66.888)

—Jane Marshall

© 1992 Hope Publishing Co., Carol Stream, IL 60188. All rights reserved.

Ode to Joe
and most other basses of my acquaintance

(Previously unpublished)

When basses make their feelings known
    (that's frequently), they're heard to moan,
"Why must we climb the upper half
    of what's regarded as 'our' staff?
Leave that for baritones to use,
    or, if you must, the Tenor Twos;
The populace by now should know
    that basses were created low."

    Refrain:
*   Low, low, ever so low;
        let ledger lines go
    unless they're below.
        Low, low, exquisitely low:
    God's gift to the world
        is the bass voice unfurled
    To sing low, low-down, low.*

Of all the lines unfit to sing
    th'unfittest are the ones that wing
Into the vocal stratosphere
    above Line Three, where basses fear
Their shrieking, once their tune does fall,
    will leave them with no voice at all,
And thus deprive the human race
    of music's diamond: Second Bass. (Ref.)

So basses of the world, unite
 against your voice's bleakest blight:
Arrangers and composers who
 persist in tenorizing you.
Refuse those tones, stand fast, stand firm,
 and join with groundhog, mole, and worm,
With walrus, whale, and Jacques Cousteau,
 who celebrate the Great Below. (Ref.)

—Jane Marshall

© 1992 Hope Publishing Co., Carol Stream, IL 60188. All rights reserved.

Tones of Grace

Author's Note

Some notes in musical phrases are structurally less important than others, just as some words in our verbal phrases and sentences are less substantive than others. Such tones may not be the bone and flesh of the message, but at the very least they clothe the framework with warmth and richness, decorating the phrases to make them more beautiful.

Music has its names for these embellishments that grace the score and the sound: ornaments, non-basic tones, decorative pitches. Whatever their names, they enhance and ornament. Mozart without passing tones, Bach without suspensions, Verdi without trills would hardly be the Wolfgang, Johann Sebastian, and Guiseppe we know but composers very different and undoubtedly less inspiring.

Could it be that these little devices in music have their counterparts in other places, things, and ideas? In people, even?

I thought I'd take a look and see.

PASSING TONE: *a tone or tones connecting two basic pitches by a stepwise motion.*

In a passage *do, re, mi, fa, sol* for instance, *do, mi* and *sol* are the basic tones that, to musicians, form a chord. *Re* and *fa* are the passing tones or the "outsiders" that don't belong to the chord but that connect *do* with *mi* and *sol*.

A passing tone, like all decorative or non-basic tones, is not really a member of the chordal family of tones. Seasoning the musical stew sometimes sweetly, sometimes stringently, a passing tone invariably enriches and enhances the flavor of the sound. Having performed music in which there are passing tones, one cannot afterward even conceive of that particular musical delight without the passing notes that have become a part of it, foreigners though they may have been at the outset.

Any musician who has performed Handel's *Messiah* has made friends gratefully with a passing tone. Were it not for those tones in the brisk, sixteenth-note passages that festoon the score like colored chains on a Christmas tree, we would be leaping from basic tone to basic tone like Mexican jumping beans. What's more important, *Messiah*, without those delicate stepladders of sound, would not be *Messiah* at all, nor would it be Handel's.

Like those bricks Katy Henry's daddy put in his garden. To us third-graders Mr. Henry was a giant, tall, six-foot-plus arrangement of looseleaf lankiness whose stride was so long we had to run to stay beside him on his daily expeditions out to the rear of the lot, where every rainy spring he planted his vegetable garden. He had placed some large flagstones in that damp ground on the way to the tomatos and the corn, but the distance between them was measured by his long legs, not by our short ones. So, after seeing us jumping from flagstone to flagstone and frequently missing so that we landed in the mud, he got busy and gathered up some old bricks from around the neighborhood—in vacant lots, off the street, or any other place that seemed handy—and set them down between the flagstones so that we could continue to watch his garden grow without muddying up our shoes and infuriating our mothers. Passing tones those bricks were, and Katy's dad was their composer. He made our pilgrimage out to the garden infinitely smoother.

In the early days of our little church we had two separate buildings, one that housed the choir room and sanctuary and the other that housed the church offices and school classrooms. The unroofed space outside between the two buildings was not much wider than a neighborhood street, but getting across it in the rain left us looking like newly-baptized—by immersion—wet laundry, once we got into the sanctuary. In the cold, wintry, windy weather we nearly froze, because that space was like a north-south wind tunnel. Eventually the church joined the two buildings so that the open space became the atrium or large foyer that was the official entrance to both the buildings. More importantly, the atrium became a gathering place, housing a coffee pot, an area for parish notices, a wall on which art could be hung, sometimes providing space for small group meetings, suppers, or luncheons. The atrium turned out to be decorative, but a very important part of that building, not only architecturally but socially—a true passing tone.

Colors are used as passing tones in painting.

Michelangelo, in his extraordinary fresco, "The Creation of Adam," painted on the ceiling of the Sistine Chapel, focuses on the principal points of interest—God, Adam, and the almost-touching fingers of the two—by changing colors. The changes are extreme in some places and subtle and slight in others, but these bridges of color always serve to move the eye of the viewer from one basic figure or area to another, never calling attention to themselves in the process.

Trains, passenger and freight, have passing tones, too.

I always loved trains and still revel in the memories of trips taken on them to visit grandparents in the summer. Passenger trains pulled by giant steam locomotives and fueled by coal, dragged sleeping cars, baggage cars, and the diner behind them at the breakneck speed of 60 miles an hour. To me, passenger trains were one of the marvels of the world.

Among the most delectable of the many adventures we kids delighted in on those pilgrimages were our trips through the train itself to the dining car, invariably many cars removed from our sleeper. The trips required that we negotiate those scary links of outside platforms between cars, where the floor moved, the wind threatened our balance, and the roar of the engine and wheels deafened even our squeals of half-fright, half-thrill.

Platforms were fast-moving, jiggling passing tones of transport, excitingly dissonant in their scariness as they moved us into the cozy consonance of each car leading toward the diner. They are definitely one reason the word "train" is still music to my ears.

NEIGHBOR TONE: *a decorative pitch that moves a step above or below and returns to basic pitch. In a passage like do-re-do, re is the neighbor tone; or in the other direction, do-ti-do, ti is the neighbor tone.*

A neighbor tone can decorate the musical phrase in such a way that it establishes the characteristic of that phrase. Think of the first three notes of "Silent Night," for instance. Without that second little note that goes away from, and comes back to, the basic tone, "Silent Night" simply wouldn't be "Silent Night," would it? And it wouldn't be quite as lovely.

Places can be neighboring tones and very welcome ones at that. I had an illness once that kept me homebound for almost two years because the symptoms of it were so strange that I didn't dare get away from home and stay very long, as I had been used to doing in my teaching. Besides that, the medication was so powerful and had to be so carefully monitored that I needed to stay relatively close to home so that in case of emergency I could get help quickly. So when I began to get better, the doctor said, "I think it's time now that you start traveling again in your teaching; but you might start in a modest way." Well, how does one do that? I decided that I would go short distances, either places that were close enough that I could go and come back in one day, or places at least in neighboring states, that I could get to rather quickly, spending perhaps one night, and then leaving the next day. It really worked very well; I could do my work. Though I wasn't up to full steam, I could at least build toward full steam gradually. I have always been grateful to all of those "neighbor" tone friends who didn't live so far away that I was prevented from being with them and working with them.

A neighbor tone is like what we see on an oscilloscope—that little piece of technology with a screen that shows us a picture, for instance, of a steady heartbeat, where the line runs straight then all of a sudden shows a little bump. The little bumps seem to be like neighbor tones. When they are of the same height and occur at regular intervals, they indicate a healthy heart.

An oscilloscope also measures the vibrato in the voice. I remember my days in music school when one of our teachers with his oscilloscope let us see on a screen how much vibrato we had in our voices. We got the same kind of picture. (It wasn't quite so even for me as that steady heartbeat picture was). Again those little bumps along that steady line were neighbor tones. They always went up and came back—always returned.

One thinks of a toddler just learning to walk in a room full of relatives at Christmastime—some of those relatives perfect strangers to the little one. The toddler ventures away from mother and teeters out to the middle of the room, then, looking around at all of those strange faces, manages to turn around and head right back to mother. A neighbor tone doesn't go far and always returns.

And I think of choir members who sit between other choir members who might be said to be the "basic tones" of that particular section. The neighbor tones may not have strong voices, and they may wander a little bit, but if they anchor themselves between strong voices, they contribute to the whole ensemble of sound in such a way that the sound would be different were they not there. Neighbors.

The classic neighbor, of course, was the Good Samaritan. Weren't there several others of the "inside" crowd who passed by the man in the ditch on the other side of the road and did not stop to help him out? Wasn't it a Good Samaritan, i.e., an "outsider"—one that didn't belong to the right crowd—who stopped and not only helped the man, but came back and followed up to see that the man was tended to properly before going on his way? Neighbor tones, like Good Samaritans, can be outsiders, but they can certainly be close friends and carriers of grace. And the interesting thing about the Good Samaritan is that we remember him, whereas those other folks who passed by on the other side are nameless.

Neighbor tones decorate our lives—enrich, enhance, and ornament them.

TRILL: *an ornament consisting of rapid alternation of a given pitch with the diatonic second interval above it.*

I can hardly think of trills in music without thinking of Lily Pons. When I was growing up, Lily Pons was one of the reigning coloraturas at the Met. She was a diminutive woman, less than five feet tall. I never knew her, yet I was always awed by the kind of singing that she did. I remember very well those coloratura roles, *Lucia di Lammermoor* and *Lakme*, that she made so famous. I always waited, holding my breath, for Lily to get to those high notes in the cadence figures where she trilled before ending each aria. In opera particularly, the trills multiply because the purpose is to show off the virtuoso ability of the performer.

Another one of my favorite pieces of music has a kind of hidden trill in it, but, in my particular old vinyl recording, the trill can be heard very clearly in the overture to *Die Meistersinger*. It occurs in the horns, where one doesn't hear trilling very often. The fast little flutter sounds rather strange coming from a french horn.

I think also of Brahms' monumental *First Piano Concerto*. Before the first phrase is ever completed there is a trill. That whole concerto actually is characterized by long trills, sometimes by both hands.

The tops of birthday cakes frequently have colored designs created by one of those icing squirt guns. The designs are absolutely unessential to the taste of the cake but a requisite for attractiveness. They say trillingly that they are helping to celebrate a festive occasion.

Tuxedo shirts are full of trills because many of them, at least at the time I am writing these words, have ruffles down the front. When I was growing up, a man didn't wear a tux shirt with ruffles, but ruffles have become standard since. Some of them are even etched with a little black strip all the way down either side. The ruffles are functionally unnecessary, but they're decorative. They add something very special and festive to tuxedo attire.

Trills exist in choirs in the form of people. There are nearly always a couple of cut-ups in any choir—you're lucky if you have just two—who play off each other, frequently cracking funny jokes and coming out with hilarious comments, sometimes in the most unexpected places in rehearsal. Without those "trills"—those two folks alternating back and forth with the crazies—choir rehearsal would not be nearly as much fun.

Does anybody not know what it feels like to be in love or to be so happily moved by something that one can feel one's heart flutter? We even have a musical term for that: we say "skipped a beat" to indicate a rapid alternation. When the heart flutters healthily, something is happening that is beautiful to the soul.

We need trills, even though they are classed as unessential. But since they beautify, can we actually say they are unessential?

PEDAL POINT: *a long note that continues to sound as harmonies change in other parts.*

Pedal points are all over the place in music, so much so that we almost take them for granted, like the passing tone. One thinks immediately of Bach's organ *Toccata in F* that starts with a low "F" in the pedal, over which the toccata begins, grows, intensifies, and gets more complex measure after measure while that low "F" continues.

And, of course, there is the Brahms *Requiem* with its famous low "D" pedal point in the movement in which the choir sings about the righteous being in the hands of God. Those double bass players bow away on that low "D" for 18 pages of the full score while all kinds of harmonies and rhythms occur above it in the orchestral and voice parts.

An inverted pedal point is one that is in a higher voice, not necessarily the bass part or the pedal—usually a very high voice or instrument. There is one in the familiar wedding march in Mendelssohn's *Midsummer Night's Dream* incidental music. Most folks don't hear it because when the organist plays it at a wedding he or she doesn't come to the pedal point until almost the end of that wonderful recessional. By that time the crowd is out of the church.

Pedal points show up other places, too. I think of this every time I look out the window on cold December days at my Carolina jessamine, which keeps on blooming regardless of the season. It's cold, damp, and rainy outside as I write this and another freeze is predicted, but the Carolina jessamine refuses to quit. It may close down for a while, but, even in cool weather, it returns.

We think of hills and mountains as being everlasting. We speak of the "eternal hills." But look at the Grand Canyon. What is eternal about the Grand Canyon is the Colorado River, not the hills. Like a pedal point, the river moves along in time and gradually cuts through layer after layer of those ancient mountains.

One thinks of Shakespeare and the English language. What a pedal point! Styles change in language, but somehow the cadences of Shakespeare continue to move us. We make changes in our speech to accommodate the times very frequently, but somehow we're less willing to change Shakespeare. It's a comfort to know that there are some unchanging qualities among the many upheavals in our lives—even in the language.

The Constitution is a pedal point in our government. Amendments can be made above it. Laws and statutes evolve, but the Constitution remains the pedal point of our life together as a republic.

Not everything has to be a profound pedal point. Take my friend Patty's baking pan, for instance. That pan is distorted. It's bent. It's black. It's about the most unattractive piece of equipment I have seen in a kitchen, and this in the kitchen of one of the best cooks I know. She says she has had the pan 30 years and she is not about to change it. (That's her version of "If it ain't broke, don't fix it.") I suppose there have been thousands of cookies, dozens and scores of pieces of baked chicken, and brownies, fudge, and biscuits by the barrel that have come out of that pan—all wonderful. Very few brides in their right minds these days would be caught dead with a pan that is as disreputable as Patty's pan. Patty has changed kitchens over the years and changed recipes, but the pan lingers. It looks awful, but it produces something beautiful.

People can be pedal points that refuse to quit, regardless of the changing circumstances around them. I think of Beethoven. He was deaf, of course—stone deaf—when he wrote the *Ninth Symphony*, and yet there's as much life in that work and as much genius as there is in his *First Symphony*. How can that be? It is beyond imagination.

I had a letter recently from the son of the late great Christian minister, Toyohiko Kagawa of Japan, who was known for his work among the poor and on behalf of labor unions and the oppressed in Japan at the time of World War II. Because he opposed the Japanese war policy, he was thrown into jail twice during the '40s. Mr. Kagawa Sr. died many years ago, but his son, who was the person writing me to grant permission to set a text of his father's to music, tells me that he has been choir director since 1939 at the Christian church in Japan which his father founded. I write this in 1990. Fifty-one years is a long time for a choir director or anyone to serve in one place. He is active in the local hymn society and is an involved musician making beautiful things happen. I'd call him a pedal point.

Then there's my Aunt Dollie Fakes. Aunt Dollie lived to be 102. She was a delightful old lady, full of fun. She had been a very beautiful young woman who still retained her twinkle and much of her beauty even at 100 years of age. She never wanted to tell her age until she reached that mark. Then she realized she was something extraordinary, so she was quite willing to let everybody know how old she was. One of her favorite stories was that all of the pallbearers she had chosen had died and the dress she had picked out to be buried in had rotted. I can hear her cackle now with glee and shake with laughter as she told that story.

My 94-year-old mother, named for Aunt Dollie, is a carbon copy of her. And my mother, with the same kind of wit and love of people and life, shows every sign of matching Aunt Dollie's longevity record. Both of them would be the first to say that their bodies may die but that's not the end of them by a long shot. And I believe that because they say so.

Pedal points may be non-basic tones, but how they do enrich our lives and our music. How nice to know that there are constants among all of our variables. They may be purely stubborn; they may be simply secure. But they refuse to quit. They are just like that river cutting through the Grand Canyon or that other old river, the Mississippi, which just "keeps rolling along." All praise for pedal points!

A**PPOGGIATURA:** *a non-basic melodic tone approached by leap and left by step in the opposite direction.*

Appoggiaturas abound, but the first musical one that I think of occurs in "O Little Town of Bethlehem" at the end of the second line, when we sing "the silent stars go by." The note on "stars" is an appoggiatura. You get to it by jumping to it from another tone, which is a basic tone, but you leave it by going stepwise to another basic tone in the opposite direction.

Appoggiaturas abound in life, too. One thinks of the famous moonwalk in 1969—an appoggiatura on a grand scale. What a leap those astronauts took from earth to the moon! But do you remember the pictures of them coming out of the capsule and descending, ever so gently, onto the nearby surface of the moon? I'd call that a form of cosmic appoggiatura.

Skyrockets on the Fourth of July are appoggiaturas in color, shot out of their source, leaping into the night sky, but then descending quietly, until they quickly disappear.

Many scientific discoveries qualify as appoggiaturas. The scientist takes a great leap of imagination and happens onto something that turns out to be mindboggling. What comes after that discovery, however, is painstaking research and documentation and proof and testing before that scientific discovery actually becomes a part of our lives. Scientific appoggiaturas abound.

I think of those Wise Men we read about in Matthew's gospel. They were outsiders. They didn't belong to the folks known as the chosen people, and they came from a long way off—from the East (with a capital "E," the Bible says—biblical talk for a "long way off"). They represented the whole Gentile world. What a leap of faith they took to get to the manger in Bethlehem! But they left by stepping their way cautiously, the Bible says, onto another route. They took a different road because of what they had discovered as a result of their great leap of faith into the unknown.

Our mountaintop experiences are similar. The transfiguration story that is so fascinating and so puzzling sends us in one bound into the stratosphere where, like Peter and his friends, we catch a vision of something remarkable. That vision was over as quickly as it had come. What happened afterwards was the trek, step by step, down the mountain. Sometimes we experience mountaintop events by a great leap of imagination or faith, but what follows is nearly always a step-by-step trudge down from that event into our own world, where shirtsleeves must be rolled up and we must get back to the Monday morning business of living and serving.

ESCAPE TONE: *a non-basic tone approached by step and left by leap in the opposite direction.*

An escape tone (or appoggiatura in reverse) that occurs to me in musical language happens in the aria, "He Shall Feed His Flock" from Handel's *Messiah*, at the end of the first section: "and he shall carry the young lambs in his arms." Of the last few notes ("in his arms"), *e, f, d, c*,—the *f* is the *echapee*, as it's known in French (and in crossword puzzles), an escape tone.

Escape tones are nearly always of short duration, as are some of the other non-chord tones, but they still decorate, enrich, and enliven everything around them. We call some travel escape, and indeed it can be. If, on the other hand, we keep escaping by traveling first to one place and then another and another, and never stay home when we could, the travel becomes something other than a decoration. It becomes a way of life. Escape, then, may be more *de*structive than *con*structive.

I could be tempted easily to get into my favorite mystery novels, read all day, and get nothing done. I suppose they are called "escapes," but if I spent too much time in those novels they get to be much more than a short duration "escape" tone. They take me away from things that I should be doing. Certainly we know that television can turn us into couch potatoes rather than human beings who simply enjoy TV now and then as a means, not only of information, but of escape and recreation.

But choir directors can use the escape tone idea to great effect in their rehearsal technique. If a rehearsal is constant work without relief or let-up or a break or a joke or even a change of style of music being rehearsed, it can be drudgery of the first magnitude. A wise director will use an escape tone in the form of a change-of-pace in rehearsal so that people go home relaxed rather than exhausted. I expect that the music is better learned in a rehearsal like that than in a rehearsal where everything is dead-serious all the time and people feel put-upon rather than conducted lovingly.

My husband and I have friends who like to get away from the city for very short periods of time and have built a small house over in the East Texas woods on a tiny lake. They have lovingly decorated and furnished that house so that it indeed is a wonderful geographical and architectural escape tone. They can get to it in just over an hour, leaving the busy, polluted, dirty, traffic-filled city behind, enjoy that tiny little house for a night or two in those beautiful woods on that sparkling lake, and then come back to the city refreshed.

My gin rummy is an escape tone. Everybody needs recreation. I'm not very good anymore—if indeed, I ever was good—at strenuous athletic activity. So years ago one of my friends taught me to play gin rummy. I usually lost, but the game was more fun than winning, unless, of course, I lost too many games in a row. Gin rummy, like crossword puzzles, has turned out to be for me an escape tone. It is very different from everything else I do. Most of my activity that is not family activity is musical activity and I love it, but even musical activity, if it has no relief, can acquire a sameness that can be deadly. That's where the gin rummy comes in. Maybe it's the difference between using the left brain and using the right brain. Whatever it is, it enriches and enhances my life.

I think this is true of meditation and of much of our worship. Life would be terrible drudgery and destructive if we didn't take time out to think on deeper things than we are accustomed to thinking upon. I know for a fact that composers have to have their time alone—their "head" time, as one of my friends calls it. They must have their time away from sound so that the machinery inside their heads, their ears, and their souls can be refueled and renewed.

One of the characteristics of the escape tone is that, though it may be approached by step, it is left by leap: so escape tones, in whatever form they appear in our lives, can send us leaping back into our daily routine because they have provided us with a kind of ornament that has graced those special moments and has energized us for the down-to-earthness which constitutes most of life.

ANTICIPATION: *a short, unaccented note of same pitch as the accented note it precedes and prepares for.*

Anticipations usually occur in the melody of pieces of music that we hear. Indeed, most of the other non-basic tones do, too. The suspension, I suppose, is the exception. The anticipation gets the ear ready in music for the note that is to come in the melody, for it is a little stammer ahead of the final note on the same pitch.

One thinks of the very last phrase in that familiar aria in *Messiah*, "He Shall Feed His Flock," where the phrase ends, "that are with young." The note on "with" is the same note that occurs on "young" in that aria, preparing the ear for the final tone.

Music of that particular period is full of anticipations. I think also of Jeremiah Clarke's "Prince of Denmark March," so frequently used now as a processional at weddings. The last measures of that well-known melody, usually played on the organ but sometimes played by a solo trumpet, contain an anticipation, the note immediately preceding the final note. As a matter of fact, if we heard the anticipation note and the music suddenly stopped, we would know without any question what the last note in the melody was to be.

Anticipations occur elsewhere, too. One of my favorite anticipations was, and is, the dasher in the freezer that my husband nearly always calls me to come lick after he has finished making ice cream in the summertime. (I come from a long line of ice cream freaks.) We get a big platter and together pull that ice cream-coated dasher out of the cold metal container encased in ice and whisk it quickly, so it won't drip all over the kitchen floor, onto the platter. There's not a lot of ice cream there, but the anticipation of that first taste, particularly that first batch of the summer season, is pure delight. I lick the dasher clean, and I doubt that the ice cream, good as it is, ever tastes any better than it does right then. Those few licks off the dasher get me ready for what is to come: a feast of much more of the same.

Several years ago I went with a friend to hear the Boston Symphony at Tanglewood in Massachusetts. We flew to Boston and rented a car and drove all the way across the state, west on the Massachusetts Turnpike into the Berkshires where Tanglewood is located, near the little town of Lenox. The trees were mostly green, for this was August. They were huge—bigger than the trees we have in Texas, which of course in August are completely green. But I noticed as we traveled that these trees on either side of the turnpike had little spots of rust in them, especially near the tops. I was concerned about this and said to my friend, "It must be some sort of disease. Some of the leaves seem to be dying in isolated spots among the trees near the top." She, being much better traveled than I and much wiser, said, "I have an idea that those trees are beginning to turn into their fall colors." I couldn't believe that was true and said so. "But it's only August," was my provincial comment.

We went back another year a little bit later in the month and found the trees showed bigger spots of red and rust and yellow. Clearly my friend was right. The trees were truly beginning to turn. Those little spots of rusty leaves were anticipations, forecasting what was to come very shortly in those big trees along the Massachusetts Turnpike and throughout New England. One can see simply the little spots of rust and know for sure that the end of summer is coming and that very soon will follow the brilliant, accented colors of fall. True anticipations, those rusty leaves in August.

In Texas we experience some very heavy atmosphere, particularly in the summertime, when the sky is overcast with heavy clouds, the barometer goes down, the humidity goes up, and there is no breeze of any kind. People are likely to get a little bit uneasy because the weather is uncomfortable and the barometer is low. Usually a thunderstorm clears the atmosphere and brings out the sun, sending the barometer back up. I suppose this heavy atmosphere is anticipation in a minor key, because that oppressively low barometer nearly always tells us and our animal friends that a storm is coming, after which there will be a change for the better. Anticipations can come in a minor key, too.

Almost every student of choral music knows Vaughan Williams' "O Taste and See," his lovely, simple setting for four voices of one phrase in Psalm 34. So we end our consideration of anticipations as we began it—talking about taste.

I mentioned those dashers of ice cream that anticipated the delights of desserts to come. Even in spiritual life there are anticipations. The Psalmist expresses this reality by saying, "O taste and see how gracious the Lord is. Happy are those who trust in the Lord." That's what Vaughan Williams set to music. Just a taste of grace, of ornament, of beauty, of forgiveness, of love that occurs not regularly, but as a surprise, when we least expect it and perhaps least deserve it. Just a taste tells us something about what is in store if only we can trust and wait. The anticipation is all we need to know.

I've been reminded of a counterpart that we can see rather than hear as I've walked westward early in the morning just before the sun actually peeps over the horizon. When there are clouds in the west, they light up in a beautiful pink, reflecting off the rising sun across the sky. They don't last long, but they are anticipations of that brightest light the human eye knows. Pink clouds in the western heavens in the morning, brief and light though they may be, are anticipations of something wonderful ahead: sunlight.

Poulenc, I think, knew this when he ended the *Stabat Mater*, one of his greatest choral works, not on a tonic chord, which indicates rest, repose, and finality, but on a subdominant seventh suggesting something everlasting still to come which we await in excitement, anticipation, and trust.

SUSPENSION: *a tone beginning as a basic pitch but becoming a non-basic pitch extending beyond the next rhythmic accent, either by a tie or by repetition, and then resolving by step to another basic pitch.*

In musing about suspensions one thinks, if one is a fan of Johann Sebastian Bach, of the sixth *Brandenburg Concerto*, specifically the Allegro that ends the concerto. The section is a textbook on suspensions, melodic notes not part of the inner harmonic framework that absolutely characterize that very delightful, frisky movement of a wonderful piece of music.

Suspensions, of course, occur everywhere, and I suppose they are the most graphic illustration in musical ornamentation of that principle of tension and release that is not only a part of life but certainly a part of music. Where would we be without dissonance resolving to consonance in music, that is to say, without tension that resolves eventually into release?

I remember a dear friend saying to me years and years ago, "It's almost worth having a good argument in order to get to the making-up part afterwards." The resolution, the making-up, the renewing of the deep friendship might not happen in such a poignant way were it not for the argument that preceded it. And, of course, something always leads up to the argument: the preparation.

In music, when one really wants to get clinical about the definition of suspension, one reads in the theory books that a suspension figure consists of three parts: the preparation, the suspension itself, and the resolution.

I'm reminded of my childhood days in the back yard in the swing. My swing was not just one of those put-together metal affairs that one buys and assembles, but a real swing that my father built, using great big poles—almost like telephone poles—set in concrete with a brace across the top from which he hung the swing.

I thought mine was wonderful. My friends and I who gathered in the back yard developed a whole set of stunts in which, perceiving ourselves as experts, we worked our way up to a great arc and then jumped out of the swing. We had all kinds of names for those stunts. (The "Parachute" was one.) But there was a moment, after we had prepared for the big jump by pumping ourselves up to that great arc, when we were suspended in the air with the swing falling away behind us. It was a very short suspension, but that's what provided the excitement of the whole thing. We dropped, of course, very easily to the ground, because the swing wasn't all that high, and we weren't all that big. Preparation, suspension, and resolution were all there.

We know about suspension in drama, certainly in opera, where frequently, at least in a three-act production, the suspension is prepared for and builds to the end of the second act. Nothing is resolved when the second act curtain comes down. Everything has come to some sort of very tense, electrifying moment of suspension. Even after the third-act curtain opens and figures appear on the stage, that suspense is not resolved. It is only after we move into the third act following the buildup of tension—the suspension itself—that there is a quick resolution, either tragic or joyful.

We remember learning about the form of the short story, where three quarters of the way through the action builds up to a suspension; then, all of a sudden, there is a *denouement*, a resolution, a release of the tension.

I think of suspension in many final rehearsals of choirs before an important performance, particularly of special works or extended works—something like the Vivaldi *Gloria* or the Fauré *Requiem*, for instance. The choir has worked for weeks and weeks to prepare for the occasion, but the final rehearsal is not as smooth as one would hope. Unresolved spots in the music are not yet perfected. Sometimes in that final rehearsal, particularly if the instrumentalists are present for the first time with the chorus, singers are very uncomfortable and go away thinking, "How will we ever perform this work on Sunday and make it sound as beautiful as it should be?" The suspense carries all the way through the weekend until the final performance, when more often than not the whole thing comes off much better than anyone could have predicted. The suspension is certainly prepared for ahead of time over long weeks of rehearsal, but after that final practice and point of no return, the suspense lingers on to the performance day. It is not resolved until that performance is completed—successfully, God willing.

In nature, in music, and in relationships, by some cosmic chemistry we can't understand but can only celebrate, tension and suspense and dissonance resolve into rest, release, and harmony. In those brief and magic moments we can echo Browning's Pippa:

> *God's in his heaven—*
> *All's right with the world.*

GRACE NOTE: *a very short tone attached to and preceding a more important tone but having no regular rhythmic value. A grace note is usually printed in a smaller size than the note it ornaments.*

Wasn't it fun, if you studied piano, to get a piece that had your first grace note in it? I think of the "Anvil Chorus," with those fast, repeated notes that are all embellished by grace notes while the anvils are being struck on the stage of *Il Trovatore*. One gets the feeling of something happening—no, of something getting *ready* to happen. The sound is very pleasing, even though it is supposed to imitate an anvil being struck.

Grace notes occur frequently. Have you ever had a close friend who was so in tune with you that often you both discovered yourselves saying exactly the same words at the same time? I have one like that, and over the years that phenomenon has continued. We'll be discussing something, there'll be a pause, and both of us will start speaking simultaneously with exactly the same idea. We simply laugh. Underneath that laugh and that look there are those long years of relationship—a grace note enriching our relationship immeasurably.

A grace note happened to me once when I visited the National Art Gallery in Washington, where I quite unexpectedly came upon a small Vermeer. I saw it from a great distance because it was on a stand with lights trained on it in a room at the end of a long corridor. One could approach that room from a long distance and see that beautiful painting, small though it was, like a little jewel in the darkness. If you know Vermeer, you know that many of his paintings are studies in the use of light coming through a window. That painting is a notable example. My heart skipped a beat, and I've never forgotten the moment. That grace note of art enriched my life then, and the memory of it still does.

On my dressing table is a smooth stone, a rock, that one of my dear musician friends gave to me many years ago. It was special to him. I forget where he got it. I even forget the story about it. The stone looks like a smoothed-off piece of lava. Though I've forgotten the particulars, I very clearly remember the feeling that I had then and the feeling that I have every day when I look at it, because he gave it to me as a token of our special friendship.

As far as my inner soul is concerned, I think of one last grace note provided by the late, great theologian and hymnologist, Erik Routley, who was such a delight to know—full of fun, erudite, witty, absolutely himself, scholar of the first rank. I remember being at Montreat at the Presbyterian Conference on Music and Worship one summer a long time ago where Dr. Routley was a member of the staff. I recall vividly an almost casual comment he made there. Whether it was stated simply to me or in a public setting I can't remember, but the quote was, "Sin is not believing God loves you." That was a grace note perhaps unessential to my physical life, but it has become an essential part of my own spiritual and emotional life. While I forget this truth again and again, I'm helped to remember it because another dear friend of mine who did beautiful cross-stitch was with me at the time we heard Dr. Routley make the comment, and she knew how much it meant to me to hear those words. So she cross-stitched a bookmark for me with "Sin is not believing God loves you," on it, and I have it standing on my dresser right against the mirror so that many times every day I can see it.

Grace notes may be short, almost inconsequential. They may have no regular rhythmic value. They occur usually as surprises. The skeleton, even the flesh, of the music would be there without them. But they ornament and embellish and grace the music, as their counterparts in all of art, nature, and society grace our very lives.

Indeed, when all is said and done, are these so-called ornamental tones of life and art really non-basic? If they are beauty in any form, could we not argue that they are essential to a wholeness of life so frequently missing in this automated and polluted world?

Others have thought so, as John Newton continually reminds us:

> *'Tis grace hath brought me safe thus far,*
> *and grace will bring me home.*